HEY,
MR PRODUCER!
THE MUSICAL WORLD OF
CAMERON
MACKINTOSH

HEY, MR PRODUCER!

THE MUSICAL WORLD OF CAMERON MACKINTOSH

SHERIDAN MORLEY AND RUTH LEON

BACK STAGE BOOKS

AN IMPRINT OF WATSON-GUPTILL PUBLICATIONS, NEW YORK

For Diana, and in memory of Ian
R. L. & S. M.

The authors wish to acknowledge gratefully all the help
they have received in the writing of this book first
and foremost from, Sir Cameron Mackintosh,
and from Nick Allott, Kathryn Bailey, Barry Burnett,
Claire Colreavy, Judith Flanders, Tee Hesketh,
Michael Le Poer Trench, Sir Andrew Lloyd Webber,
Thomas Mann, Rosy Runciman,
Karen Shaw and Bob West.

First published in Great Britain in 1998
by Weidenfeld & Nicolson

Text copyright © Sheridan Morley and Ruth Leon, 1998.
The moral rights of Sheridan Morley and Ruth Leon to be identified as the
authors of this work have been asserted in accordance with the Copyright,
Designs and Patents Act of 1988

Design and layout copyright © Weidenfeld & Nicolson, 1998

Design style by Nigel Soper

All pictures reproduced by kind permission of
Cameron Mackintosh Limited with additional pictures
supplied by the following:
© Derek Balmer: 34; © Clive Barda/Performing Arts Library: 104,
112, 112–3, 113, 114 above & below; © Donald Cooper: 38–9, 39
above & below, 50–51, 52, 80 above, 83, 87, 160–161, 161 centre;
© Glen Copus/Evening Standard: 165;
© P. Cunningham: 80 below; © Alan Davidson: 77, 115 below;
© Zoë Dominic: 37 above, 43, 82 above & below;
© Mark Douet: 176–7; © John Haynes: 84 below;
© Mike Lawn: 25; © Michael Le Poer Trench: 2, 10, 66, 68–9,
72–3, 73, 74–5, 85, 86 above, 88, 90–91, 94–5, 96, 97, 102–3, 103
all, 108, 116, 119, 120, 121 all, 122, 128 all, 130, 132–3, 133 all,
134 left, 140 above & left, 140–141, 146 background, 150, 151,
152–3, 156, 158, 159 all, 162 above right, 162–3, 163 inset 166,
167, 168–9, 169, 170, 188–9, 190, 190–191, endpapers;
© Joan Marcus: 146 inset, 153; © Bob Marshak: 92;
© Hilaria McCarthy/Daily Express: 28; © Doug McKenzie: 49
above; © The Panic Pictures Library: 41 above, 61, 64;
© Carol Pratt: 177 left & right; © Really Useful Group: all artwork
for Cats and The Phantom of the Opera; © Rex Features: 129;
© Ken Rimell/Surrey Advertiser: 30;
© Carol Rosegg/Martha Swope: 57 above & below, 58;
Robin Street/© Cameron Mackintosh Limited: 41 above right;
© Colin Willoughby/CJW Photographic: 162 below left;
Reg Wilson/© Cameron Mackintosh Limited: 54 above, 54–5, 63,
65, 70–71, 172.

Every effort has been made to contact all copyright holders. The Publishers will be
pleased to hear from any copyright holders not here acknowledged.

Published in the United States in 1998 by Back Stage Books, an imprint of Watson-Guptill Publications,
a division of BPI Communications, Inc., 1515 Broadway, New York, NY 10036-8986

Library of Congress Catalog Card Number: 98–87601

ISBN 0-8230-8816-2

Manufactured in Italy
1 2 3 4 5 6/ 03 02 01 00 99 98

CONTENTS

PREFACE

ANDREW LLOYD WEBBER

I first met Cameron Mackintosh by total happenstance. In 1978 there was a cabaret staged for London's Laurence Olivier Awards at the Café Royal. The Laurence Olivier Awards, unlike the New York Tonys, have for some reason never quite settled on their format. They can also be somewhat chaotic. You get things like the hit tune from a non-winning musical being played as the winner of another musical sprints on stage to tell an indifferent audience that his or her entire career would not have been possible without Auntie Flo or assistant choreographer Kevin.

It was through the 1978 incarnation of these awards (in those days they were called the 'Wedgies' because, for a short time, the award itself was a Wedgwood pot – the top of which came off in *Evita's* case) that I met our man Cameron.

He wanted to hit me. Tim Rice and I had won best musical for our effort about the wife of an Argentine dictator. I had, as it turned out both foolishly and fortuitously, made a comment to the effect that the shambolic cabaret staged by Sir C – not his fault, I subsequently discovered – should have been masterminded by the legendary director of our epic, Hal Prince.

Tim and I used to be managed by a guy called David Land. David, God rest his splendid soul, redefined the stereotypical, wisecracking Jewish agent. He once had a company called Hope and Glory plc, so he could pick up the phone and announce: 'Land of Hope and Glory'.

David also could fan a decent flame when he saw one. So, when he heard that Cameron was incensed by my passing stricture, he entered the fray with the bellows that only he could muster.

First, I was bemused. I didn't know Cameron Mackintosh. I knew of him only as the producer of rather canny revivals of musicals and various touring productions. I assumed he was a sixty-ish wizened Scots person, an old-timer who had got a bit peeved by an upstart like me. As I am half Scottish I thought I was well capable of dealing with the codger, and could easily schmooze the old boy with a 'sorry, my remarks must have been misunderstood' letter. This was duly dispatched and I assumed that was the end of it.

I then decided to set up my own company to produce my own work, and a couple of years later I found myself intrigued by this bloke who seemed to be the only Brit around producing musicals, and he was doing it in a particularly hyperactive mode for one clearly so old and past it. The canny chap had even got his hands on

Arts Council cash to stage such esoteric material as *My Fair Lady* and *Oklahoma!*

So I asked him to lunch at the Savile Club, an establishment of which I was a member in those days. It was next door to the offices of Robert Stigwood who had produced *Joseph* and *Jesus Christ Superstar*.

I must confess that I was unprepared for Cameron when he bounced in. This was not the wizened Scot I had envisaged. In fact the boyish, impish figure I was viewing didn't look Scottish at all. This is possibly because his delightful mother is Maltese.

It was around about drink two that the impact of our meeting walloped us: we had both met, for the first time in Britain, another person equally mental about musical theatre.

I don't remember much about the latter part of the lunch that changed both our lives. I do remember that my office phoned at around 7.30 to see that I was OK, and check that Cameron had not slugged me out cold.

I also remember telling my incredulous office next morning that I wanted Cameron to co-produce *Old Possum's Book of Practical Cats* as a musical with me.

Actually, I do remember quite a bit about the *Old Possum* part of the lunch. I remember Cameron telling me how he had gone about persuading the Arts Council to part-finance his recent musical revivals. He told me that though he'd loved the concept album of *Evita,* he hadn't cared for it as much on stage in London, but had changed his mind when he saw it in New York. He asked me about my relationship with Robert Stigwood. I told him that one of the greatest things that Stigwood had done was to get productions up and running around the world once the initial show was proven. It was but a couple of years later that Cameron and I were to learn the pluses and pitfalls of international production when we did it ourselves. No one has done it better than Cameron.

I told him about Valerie Eliot. She and Faber and Faber controlled *Old Possum*, so I told of my meeting with Valerie, after which she had granted me the rights to make a musical of her husband's work. I told him that she said Tom Eliot would not have wanted any show about cute pussy cats. He had apparently turned down an offer from Disney to make the book into an animated follow-up to *Fantasia*. Once our deal was done, Cameron hurled himself into *Cats* with the energy and certainty that are now his well known trademarks.

First port of call was Gillian Lynne, with whom he had worked on his revival of *My Fair Lady*. This was a brilliant thought. Gillian was at the time, and still is, the most experienced British choreographer of musicals. Her dance vocabulary stretches from classical ballet to jazz. She can also create really naughty stuff: Gillian is no Disney cartoon animal.

But where Cameron was clever was that he knew that if he hooked Gillian, he had a conduit to the then head honcho of the Royal Shakespeare Company, Trevor Nunn. Gillian had previously collaborated with Trevor Nunn on *Once in a Lifetime* and *The Comedy of Errors*. Both these productions had come closer to musicals that the RSC might normally have been expected to countenance.

Trevor Nunn was someone who would fully understand the importance of the words we were dealing with. Cameron was right. Trevor had to be snared.

The courting of Trevor by Cameron and myself then ensued. Trevor agreed to join us if his trusted designer friend, John Napier, could come aboard. And John would design for us only if we went into a totally unconventional theatre space. That's what Cameron wanted. Now we had a team, we had a musical.

Unfortunately we did not have the investment.

Consider this if you will. The package that Cameron and I were offering contained, first, yours truly. OK, I had been successful with Tim Rice as my lyricist, but my only effort without him had been the disastrous *Jeeves*.

Second, this was the first show that I had been involved in without Stigwood. Cameron had produced some successful revivals, but he wasn't exactly the producer of *Hair* or *Superstar*.

Third, the words were by a dead poet.

Fourth, the director was best known for his work in classical theatre, not exactly a plus for a big musical.

Fifth, we were going into the New London Theatre. Nothing, not even *Grease* starring Richard Gere, had succeeded at the New London.

Sixth, no show heavily based on dance had ever come out of Britain. That was America's preserve alone.

Finally, and worst of all, we had humans dressed as cats.

You can imagine the cackling and gleeful rubbing of hands about impending disaster when preview one of *Cats* dawned. I remember Cameron standing with me in the wings of the New London, 20 per cent of the investment still missing, surveying our bunch of kids dressed in cat costumes.

One of the girls said, 'What the hell are we doing here?' Cameron said, 'Doing a show, dear.' We all looked at each other. The first time a pussy hit the stage, as Cameron would insist on putting it, either we were in for a moment of legendary theatrical bathos or we might just earn the right to present our evening.

Cameron and I hid during that first moment. There was applause. We hid during several sequences that we both feared were nonsense. The applause grew. When Elaine Paige, standing in at the last minute for the injured Judi Dench, stopped the show literally, we clutched each other. We appeared to have a hit.

Later, it was Cameron's idea to take two quite different pieces of mine, my one-woman show *Tell Me on a Sunday* and my Paganini *Variations*, and combine them. *Song and Dance* was his title. It sums up the creativity of this most canny of producers. It was also a surprise and sizeable hit.

Once the huge success of *Les Misérables* was secure, I suppose it was inevitable that Cameron and I would somewhat go our separate ways. Although *The Phantom of the Opera* is obviously a part of what is often referred to as the trilogy of 1980s mega-musicals, Cameron's real heart, I have always felt, was in the Boublil–Schönberg musical he had made his own. I completely understand this. Both shows were too personal to both of us. *Phantom* had been written out of love for my then wife, Sarah Brightman, and, if I am being truthful, Hal Prince was not Cameron's first choice as director.

But the look of the production is one of *Phantom's* greatest assets. And the choice of designer, Maria Björnson, was entirely Cameron's.

Cameron is as fiercely ambitious as anyone I have ever met in the theatre business. But he cares about his shows. They are his babies. You don't write or produce musicals for money, as some commentators opine. You write or produce them because you love the genre. Musicals are not produced by formula. There are big-buck companies now coming into the theatre, either through exploiting properties proven in other fields, or by regarding theatre simply as a business, but these guys don't really understand what it's all about.

Shortly after Sheridan Morley asked me if I would write this preface, I had a long overdue lunch with Cameron. We spent a couple of hours talking about the current state of musicals and how corporate types had become involved in our beloved form. Cameron suddenly turned to me and said, 'You know, we needn't worry about them. When they've given up on musicals because they don't understand them, you and I will still be there doing exactly what we've always done.'

That night I woke up thinking how right he was. Cameron, it is a joy to salute you. You are a true giant of musical theatre.

INTRODUCTION

In the whole history of British stage musicals, which could effectively be seen to have started a century ago with the management of Gilbert and Sullivan by Richard d'Oyly Carte, no single producer has ever achieved the commercial, international and artistic credit of Sir Cameron Mackintosh. Still only in his early fifties, Mackintosh has been responsible, first in the West End and then throughout the world, for a stream of hits unique in the annals of show business.

From *Cats* through *Phantom of the Opera* (both managed in collaboration with their composer Andrew Lloyd Webber) to *Les Misérables, Miss Saigon*, and the, as yet, rather more commercially fragile *Martin Guerre*, Mackintosh has effectively reinvented the form. Before his time, in the forty years that had elapsed since the heyday of Noël Coward and Ivor Novello, big London musicals were, almost without exception, Broadway-based, and would make trips across the Atlantic usually only at the end of a long domestic road tour.

But if much of the West End is taken up with complaints that, as Noël Coward memorably remarked, 'The only trouble with the British is that they have never taken light music seriously enough', it is worth recalling that two of Jerome Kern's favourite collaborators on and off Broadway were the Brits P. G. Wodehouse and Guy Bolton, already in 1917 complaining that their countrymen didn't really believe that the musical theatre was in the same class as Shakespeare or Ibsen or Strindberg. Most of Coward's later musicals were written for New York rather than London, and although later composers of hit musicals, from Sandy Wilson through Lionel Bart to Antony Newley and Leslie Bricusse, were also to achieve Broadway hits, it was usually with only one or two isolated scores. However, with these few shining exceptions, between the Second World War and 1981 there was a long and fallow period in which the descriptive 'musical' barely needed the modifying 'Broadway' or 'American', so closely were the terms allied.

It was Mackintosh, aided and often abetted by Lloyd Webber, who reversed the Atlantic traffic and proved time and time again that the British (or at any rate the Anglo-French) musical could be one of the most triumphant UK exports of the 1980s and 1990s.

As a result, he is now conservatively reckoned to be worth £350 million: not altogether bad when you consider that in the run-up to *Cats*, only fifteen years ago, his company was so broke that he had to offer the creative team shares instead of salaries. Several of them now have country mansions and Knightsbridge town houses to show for it.

What follows is in no sense intended as the biography of this curiously private and modest man, who has lived most of his adult life in a very happy relationship with the theatrical photographer Michael Le Poer Trench. But it is, amazingly, the first book to look at the creative and commercial influence that Mackintosh alone now wields over the whole world of the stage musical. It is intended as a critical celebration, written with his blessing and with the invaluable resources of his own extensive archive; however the opinions expressed are entirely those of the authors and those to whom they have spoken about a unique career that is at best only half complete. In that sense, what we have here is a progress report – a half-time verdict. In the hundred years of the British stage musical there have been innumerable talented and sometimes revolutionary composers, lyricists, designers, directors and choreographers, but there have been only three producers who can honestly be said to have controlled and shaped its destiny. The first of these was Richard d'Oyly Carte, who took Gilbert,

Sullivan and the electric light into his own new Savoy Theatre in the final years of the last century; the second was Charles Blake Cochran who, between the wars, ensured that the three great composers of his time – Noël Coward, Ivor Novello and Vivian Ellis – were protected and patronized, at least in this country, by strong professional backstage management; and the third is Cameron Mackintosh.

If you nowadays were to look closely at the small print above the title on any Broadway or West End theatre programme for a musical, you would notice that the number of producers involved (now many of them multinational corporations), often almost equals the number of the cast. This clearly reduces risk in what is now a multi-million pound industry, but it also means an infinite number of boardroom decisions and producers' families sticking their oars into an already overcrowded pond. What is fascinating about Cameron and Lord Lloyd Webber (still functioning as Really Useful) is that they and they alone are the last of the single names above the titles of their shows.

Intriguingly, it was in the book *A Showman Looks On* (1944), one of Cochran's many and largely fictional autobiographies, that Mackintosh found the maxim by which he has governed his professional life. Cochran wrote, 'Advice to aspiring young producers: never put a show on for audiences; always put it on for yourself, and do it as best you can. Only then, maybe, will an audience come to see it.' Always stay true to your own taste.

Julian Slade's own cartoon of his first meeting with the young Cameron on the set of
Salad Days at the Vaudeville in 1954 – it all began with a magic piano.

1

THE MAGIC PIANO

"I remember the precise moment when I fell in love
with musicals; I was eight years old, and after a matinee
of *Salad Days* Julian Slade showed me the magic piano.
Until then I thought it was awfully silly and cissy
for grown-ups to go around singing and dancing"

❝I was very curious and I dived straight in, asking Julian how the magic piano really worked on-stage❞

S ir Cameron Mackintosh was born on 17 October 1946, the eldest of three sons of a Maltese mother, Diana, and a Scottish father, Ian. There was show business on both sides of the family. Ian was a respected jazz musician, known professionally as Spike, and here Cameron describes how his parents met during the Second World War when they were both working for ENSA, the organization for entertaining the troops. 'When he was playing with ENSA, in areas about to be occupied by the Germans, Ian would incorporate desperate Jewish musicians into his band and smuggle them to safety. Then he was blown up in the desert and unconscious for three months. He woke up in Naples and very soon met my mother, who was also involved in ENSA as the secretary to Nigel Patrick. She is wonderfully charming with nerves of absolute steel. She grew up during the war and survived the dreadful Siege of Malta. She had two years living under the bombardment with scarcely any food.'

In the early 1950s Ian ran a band known as the Troglodytes with Humphrey Lyttleton, but it was hard to support three hungry children on a trumpeter's salary and he had to abandon what was always his first love in favour of a regular pay-packet and respectability in his father's timber business. To the end of his life, even after forty years in the timber industry, if you asked Ian Mackintosh what he did, he'd reply that he played the trumpet, and it was precisely because he had been forced to give up his own professional love that he encouraged his sons to follow their hearts rather than their heads. Robert is now a record and show producer, while his

Overture – The young Cameron at home (left) and with his parents and younger brother, Robert (right). Ian was a jazzman, Diana the secretary to actor Nigel Patrick.

brother Nicky is a successful restaurateur. Talking about his parents, Cameron has said: 'I think I inherited my mother's bravado and practical cunning, and my father's absolutely *laissez-faire* attitude of enjoying life at all costs. My father was a wildly, fabulously, gregarious character and my mother still has the mentality of a thirty-five year old. My father enjoyed life far more than work, and on any excuse he'd be off to the pub to play the trumpet. It's a terrible thing to see one of your parents die, but there was something wonderful about all three sons and my mother being with him at the end.' Ian, who died in 1996, had lived just long enough to learn of his eldest son's knighthood.

Back in 1954, the West End was, as usual, alive with the sound of music from the other side of the Atlantic. British musicals were virtually invisible. Ivor Novello had been dead for three years and Noël Coward had just survived a run of rare and uncharacteristic musical flops. But suddenly there were two new names on the horizon. Both were public schoolboys and Oxbridge graduates, quintessentially English; both were aware that small was beautiful. The West End was ready for a theatre based on their belief that if we couldn't fight the Americans on their own spectacular Broadway territory, why not create a 'Little England' where musicals could be innocent, cheap and thoroughly lovable? Julian Slade had begun this new post-war revue tradition at the Bristol Old Vic; Sandy Wilson was also involved in intimate little shows at the Players Club. In these mid-1950s, both were to come good: Julian Slade's *Salad Days* and Sandy Wilson's *The Boy Friend*, opening within a few months of

each other, showed that there was a way forward for the apparently moribund British stage musical, just so long as it stayed small and subdued and, above all, not too expensive or expansive.

It was Slade's *Salad Days* which Cameron's favourite theatrical aunt Jean thought the eight-year-old boy might like. And he did. He liked it enough to bully his parents into a second visit just a couple of weeks later. At that time Slade himself was still playing the piano in the Vaudeville pit and, after the matinee, Cameron, before anybody could stop him, ran down the aisle, introduced himself to the surprised composer, asked to sit at the keyboard and demanded to be told all the secrets of the magic piano, which in the show sent all London dancing. Years later he still remembered the excitement of it all: 'I was very curious and I dived straight in, asking Julian how the magic piano really worked on-stage. He opened it up and showed me it was only a dummy with cups of tea inside; he said they mimed it on-stage while he played the real piano in the pit. This suddenly made sense, and then he showed me how the magic flying saucer was all done with wires; so I poked around the stage of *Salad Days* and thought I'd really like to do this when I grew up. It seemed like fun.'

Slade was now to become Cameron's honorary godfather. Very soon the boy was writing musicals for himself and his brothers which would be solemnly typed by his aunt Jean (there was no lack of supportive relatives) who worked in a City bank. Tickets were printed on a John Bull child's home-lettering set, and Cameron would dragoon his family into sitting through hour-long shows complete with numbered seats and even usherettes, made up of neighbouring schoolgirls.

A couple of years later he was sent away to boarding school at Prior Park College in Bath. Ironically, the school had once been famous for its drama productions, until a brilliantly talented but over-ambitious drama teacher, Headley Goodall, had nearly bankrupted them with lavish sets and costumes; so by the time the young Cameron arrived, end-of-term theatricals had been all but discontinued. Nevertheless his theatricality soon earned him the dormitory nickname of Darryl F. Mackintosh (since Zanuck was the most flamboyant of the current crop of Hollywood studio chiefs): 'I suppose it sounds very cocky now, but at the time I really wasn't; other boys in the class were saying they wanted to be astronauts or nuclear scientists – I just said I was going to be a producer, it all seemed that simple.'

It took him no time to persuade the relevant masters that even if they could no longer afford major school productions, they could surely

still do the occasional small-scale revue. Cameron had also had the revolutionary idea that tickets to end-of-term shows could actually be sold rather than given away to long-suffering parents as usual: 'As I needed to raise money to hire lighting and props for the end-of-term revue I got people to pay a shilling if they booked in advance, but if they left it until the night they would have to pay two on the doors; it was my first experience of managing a box-office and I used to beg scenery and costumes from the local theatres. By the time I was fourteen, I was already effectively running the Prior Park drama programme.'

At seventeen, in 1964, Cameron left school, having agreed to fulfil his parents' hopes of a university degree. Mackintosh was initially enthusiastic, largely because Julian Slade had pointed out that the undergraduate life was where both he and Sandy Wilson had devel-

1963 – The young impresario (note the Darryl F.) stages his first major production for Prior Park College. He was not yet seventeen.

By the time I was fourteen, I was already effectively running the Prior Park drama programme

oped their skills for writing musicals. But there were only two universities at that time with fully fledged drama departments – Manchester and Bristol – and as far as Cameron was concerned nothing else would do. He was, however, not very academic, and when his exam results came out it became clear that he couldn't offer the As or at the very least high Bs demanded by both universities.

Instead it was decided by the family that his best bet would be the stage-management course at the Central School of Speech and Drama. This was not, to put it mildly, a great success. 'I was accepted, and I got my grant, but as soon as I started I realized that I was never going to fit into the course. I was terribly anxious to get on and do it, but they kept telling me I would have to learn about Euripides and the historical past, whereas all I really cared about was the next band-call and whether I could get in somewhere backstage and start learning what it was all about.' It was a mismatch, a school trying to impart academic theory to a student whose only interests were practical and defined. Unlike most teenagers, Cameron knew exactly what he wanted to do, and nothing that Central could teach him would help him to start doing it. So less than halfway through his time at Central, having stuck it as long as he could, he dropped out and there is no evidence that the authorities begged him to stay. (Another producer, Richard Pillbrow, had managed only three months.) 'I lasted only a year on the stage management course because the guy who ran it kept telling me to be authoritative and to shout a lot. I have always found it much easier to smile, be charming and softly spoken, although I am accused of interfering constantly in every aspect of my productions. It seems to me that's what makes a producer.'

In any event, he now went in search of gainful and immediate employment, anything so long as it was in a theatre, backstage and hands-on. This, however, proved considerably more difficult than he had anticipated, and it was only after a dozen stage-doorkeepers had told him there was nothing available in the way of work that he found himself outside the Theatre Royal, Drury Lane, the crucible of the musical theatre, the one place on earth where he most wanted to work. Here again he had been told that there were no jobs, but at that moment, as at the Vaudeville almost exactly ten years earlier, lightning struck. As he was walking dejectedly out of the Lane and along the Colonnade, the props manager ran after him to say that there was suddenly a two-week vacancy if he could start that very night.

The show then in residence was Alan Jay Lerner and Frederick Loewe's *Camelot*, starring Paul Daneman (who was later to become Cameron's lead in *Bell, Book and Candle*) and Elizabeth Larner. 'They liked me enough that I stayed backstage there on props for five months; you only got £7 a week for eight shows, but I managed to make another £7 by volunteering to work in the mornings cleaning the foyer carpets and polishing all the brass around the dress circle. The trouble was that I have always hated getting up early, so I used to bribe a friend to go along and just plug in the Hoover, so that the theatre manager, George Hoare, would hear the noise and assume I was already at work.' Only a true-born entrepreneur would have thought of that one.

THEATRE ROYAL

BATH

Lessee and General Manager: Frank G. Maddox

PHONE 3700

Box Office open 10 a.m. to 8. p.m.

Week commencing MONDAY, MAY 5th, 1969

Evenings at 7-30   Matinee: Wednesday at 2-30   Saturday at 5-30 & 8-15

Prices: Lower Circle and Boxes 9/6, Stalls 8/6, Upper Circle Centre Block 7/6, Wings 6/6, Balcony (unres.) 3/6

CAMERON MACKINTOSH PRODUCTIONS LTD.

and

C. M. DUFF

present

A NEW PRODUCTION

of

AGATHA CHRISTIE'S

FAMOUS MURDER MYSTERY

BLACK COFFEE

featuring

VIOLA LYEL *as "AUNT CAROLINE"*

JOHN MARTIN *as "CAPTAIN HASTINGS"*

and

TERENCE DUFF *as "HERCULE POIROT"*

with

PENELOPE CHARTERIS	JENNIFER HALES	VANESSA RICHES
TERRY O'SULLIVAN	GUY GRAHAM	KEVIN FRAZER
KENNETH KEYTE	HUGH WESTWOOD	EDWARD GRANVILLE

Produced by PATRICK DESMOND

"MAIS OUI, LE CAFE NOIR, C'EST MAGNIFIQUE, VIVE MADAME CHRISTIE!"

—LE MONDE

1969 – The newborn CM Productions Company was nothing if not economical; Patrick Desmond, director of this tour of Agatha Christie's *Black Coffee*, also turns up on this poster as co-producer C.M. Duff, and star Terence Duff. It is also him in the photograph. The quote at the bottom, ostensibly from *Le Monde*, seems more likely to have been the creation of Monsieur Mackintosh's already highly developed sense of publicity hype.

2

KING ARTHUR TO THE KENTON

"Where once there was a spot, for one brief, shining moment, that was known as Camelot"

'*I really was quite terrible: the healthiest and chubbiest over-made-up workhouse orphan you have ever known*'

oon after he had gone to work backstage at Drury Lane, Cameron discovered all kinds of other jobs available there for a likely lad with boundless energy (at least after midday), unquenchable enthusiasm and a genuine, desperate desire to learn everything about the nightly making and remaking of a hit show.

In that sense, it was not just *Camelot* but the whole of the Theatre Royal, Drury Lane which gave Cameron, in only a few months and still before his twentieth birthday, a virtually complete education in musical theatre. Soon he'd graduated from props to a kind of deputy assistant stage manager, doing everything backstage from helping the actors with their many quick costume changes to riding one of the miniature hidden bicycles that propelled the horses on stage for the joust and tournament scenes. He was, however, fired from this particular job: 'You had to climb in under the stage horse and pedal like mad; one matinee I inadvertently rammed it into the proscenium arch and, assuming I was already off-stage, stuck my head out through the horse's legs, only to see 2,000 people staring at me in some amazement.' He finished up at Drury Lane washing and polishing the glasses in the dress circle bar, a safer, if less spectacular, job.

The importance to Mackintosh of these initial months at Drury Lane is beyond expression. A quarter of a century later, when, for the very first time, he took one of his own productions, *Miss Saigon*, into that theatre, it was perhaps the greatest night of his life. The boy apprentice had come home as king.

When his time at Drury Lane came to an end, there were two jobs on offer. One was to go out on the road with *Camelot* as assistant stage manager, the other was to go across to the New (now Albery) Theatre where they were rehearsing for the tour of *Oliver!* He chose the latter. 'I remember to my everlasting embarrassment on the first day I joined *Oliver!* they made us two new ASMs compete for what they said was a wonderful chance to act on the stage as part of the crowd. My voice turned out to be louder than that of the other guy though way off-key, but it meant that I had to be one of the chorus, do all the technical stuff backstage, look after huge numbers of children and operate all the radio mikes while running the show from the prompt corner. It really was an amazing education, the greatest chance in the world to do everything, and rather like being paid to go to school.'

The one thing he learned in all this was that he was one of the worst actors even he had ever seen, 'I really was quite terrible: the healthiest and chubbiest over-made-up workhouse orphan you have ever known. But to be a part of a musical that really worked, and to see it every day and night from both sides of the footlights – that is something I have never forgotten, and *Oliver!* really explains my passion for musicals.'

Although he was of course a schoolboy queuing for a shilling ticket in the gallery when *Oliver!* first opened, too young ever to have been a part of the original creative team, there is no doubt that this has been the key musical of the Mackintosh career. Time and again he revived it on the road, and as the line producer on Broadway (although there it was none too successful, in a rapidly put together production for Jimmy Nederlander); finally, in 1995, he

Cameron, assistant stage manager on the 1965/6 national tour of Lionel Bart's *Oliver!*, finds himself co-opted on stage as an extra for the crowd scenes – his first and last professional appearance as an actor.

22

brought it back in triumph to the London Palladium, having not only acquired 50 per cent of the rights from the show's many subsequent owners, but also handed a generous percentage back to his beloved Lionel Bart, the creator of the show and the man who had been driven to sell it outright in the 1970s in one of his many periods of financial collapse.

So Cameron went out on his first road tour. As assistant stage manager on *Oliver!* he earned his spurs in a somewhat understaffed backstage crew, with Ian Albery as technical director. For the first time he worked an automated prompt corner, learning the split-second timing essential for avoiding on-stage accidents. Once he was seconded to the flies high above the stage at the King's Theatre, Southsea, where all the scenery is controlled by counterweights. This nearly cost him his life when, flying in a heavy flat, he caught his hand while undoing a rope releasing a counterweight which then flew him abruptly up against the lighting grid. Had it been a smaller piece of scenery he would at the very least have been very severely concussed. This, he realized, was a highly skilled and even dangerous job, and one that, as the other flymen in the crew cut him down, Cameron made a mental note always to respect, but never again to repeat.

On his return to London, Cameron rapidly graduated to the role of deputy stage manager on a rather more short-lived musical at the Palace Theatre called *110 in the Shade* which was based on the American classic *The Rainmaker*. 'By now, I had set myself a Five-Year Plan: assistant stage manager, then deputy stage manager, then company manager and then producer. It seemed to me, God knows why, that I could do the whole thing in about five years. As things turned out, I did it in less than three.'

During the run of *110 in the Shade*, Cameron met a young man called Robin Alexandar who was in partnership with Hubert Woodward, a veteran variety agent and producer who was

1967 – Cameron goes into management with Robin Alexandar; the youngest management in Britain, not so much a *tour de force* as forced to tour, they devised the amazing travelling cheque.

Cameron Mackintosh, left, and Robin Alexandar in Newcastle yesterday.

Youngest in the business

By Journal Reporter

BRITAIN'S youngest theatre management will be bringing a new production of "Jane Eyre" to the Theatre Royal, Newcastle, next month.

The partners in Ariadne (Theatrical Managers) Ltd. are Robin Alexandar, aged 24, and Cameron Mackintosh, ...

associated with such musicals as "Oliver," "Camelot" and "Hello Dolly."

The company for "Jane Eyre" includes Jeremy Hawke, the television comedy actor, who has recently appeared with Benny Hill, and Caroline Hunt, niece of Sir John Hunt, the Everest expedition chief.

In addition to presenting the play, Mr. Alexandar ... the set... he is at ...

a four-week provincial tour which may include Newcastle.

It is based on Oscar Wilde's story, "The Portrait of Dorian Gray," and, says Mr. Mackintosh, it will be one of the most spectacular musicals ever staged.

It will cost between £80,000 and £100,000 to stage, but they have already raised a fair amount of the necessary finance and have no fears about getting the rest.

In spite of their youth, the two men say: "We think we know enough now to present ...

KENTON THEATRE
SUMMER SEASON

A Season of Five Plays in repertory presented by Hubert Woodward in association with Robin Alexander and Cameron Mackintosh.

June 26th—July 1st

The Reluctant Debutante
by William Douglas Home
A witty sophisticated comedy.

July 3rd—8th

Dial M for Murder
by Frederick Knott.
One of the best ever thrillers.

July 10th—15th

Five Finger Exercise
by Peter Shaffer
How a handsome German tutor upsets a middle-class family.

July 17th—22nd

The Chiltern Hundreds
by William Douglas Home.
The well-known comedy in which the Butler knows all.

July 25th—29th

The Knack
By Anne Jellicoe.
The knack is the knack of getting girls—those who have it and those who don't!

already into his eighties. They hired Cameron to work as a publicist (about the only job he had not yet done in the theatre) on a so-so tour of *Jane Eyre*, starring Jeremy Hawk. At this time the urbane playwright and inventor of *Desert Island Discs*, Roy Plomley, approached the Woodward–Alexandar management with the idea of reopening the Kenton Theatre in Henley-upon-Thames. This enchanting near-riverside Georgian theatre has always had a

time I really got billed as a producer.' He was still only twenty-one.

The Kenton season even made a little money, enough to confirm to Cameron that this was to be his future. Others of his management generation, Paul Elliott, Duncan Weldon and Bill Kenwright, had also by now begun to learn their trade backstage or as actors, but Cameron was the first to take off on his own.

'I worked with Robin Alexandar, at first

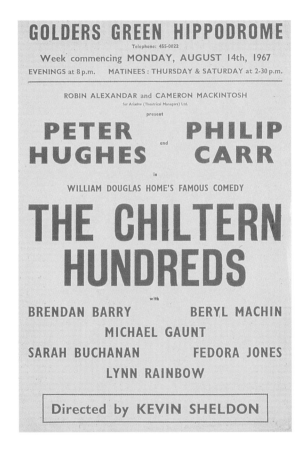

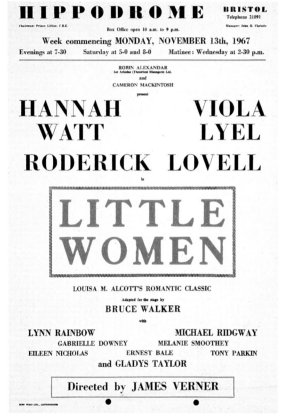

troubled financial history. Now, it is mainly used by local amateur groups but then, in 1968, local supporters had put up a guarantee of £500 a week to finance a summer season of five plays: 'We were asked to be the management, and although I had no actual experience of managing anything, it seemed to me that I was doing as much work for the Kenton as Robin and Hubert. I was also very noisy around the office, and to shut me up they put my name on the posters, so that was the first

under the paternal eye of Hubert Woodward. We set up a company called Ariadne Ltd. Our plan was to do small-scale tours at a time when you could still get a show on for around £250. I suppose you could call them tatty tours, but it was a wonderful experience having straight plays going up and down the land for six months on end.' The first of these was *Little Women*, followed later by William Douglas-Home's old West End hit *The Chiltern Hundreds*. '*Little Women* was transferred to the West End, my first ever show to do so. Even at that time I already wanted to do musicals, so I talked Robin into trying to put on a musical of *Dorian Gray* which would have cost £80,000. Mercifully, it never happened.'

Dorian Gray is one of those perennial ideas which, along with *Rasputin* and *Cyrano* (as those of us who judge musical awards know all too well), come around at least once every five years without, as yet, ever once having become a hit. For the lead Cameron wanted an actor represented by a young agent called Barry Burnett. Barry, only two years older than Cameron, was already also steeped in show business, being the son of the legendary night-club owner of the Stork Club, Al Burnett.

'One morning,' recalls Burnett, 'soon after I had set up my first office, a man phoned, identified himself as the producer, Cameron Mackintosh, and enquired as to my client's availability for *Dorian Gray*. Rather snootily I said I'd have to read the script, and he promised to send it round. A couple of hours later there was this boy standing in the office who I took to be Mr Mackintosh's messenger. I told him to leave the script on the desk and I'd get around to reading it later. Indignantly, he pointed out that he was, in fact, Mr Mackintosh. "But how old are you?" I asked in amazement. "Twenty-two," he said, "how old are you?" In that moment we started a friendship that has been one of the most important and enduring of both our lives.'

At that time the Burnett agency was in two rooms on Piccadilly, facing Fortnum and Mason. The rent came to £10 a week, quite a burden for a young agent, and while the *Dorian Gray* project came to nothing, the friendship with Barry led to Cameron later moving into Barry's second office. 'Somehow,' says Burnett now, 'I never seemed to get Cameron's share of the rent, but he used to take me to lunch at the downstairs bar at Fortnum's about three times

a week. I never have worked out how he managed to pay for that, but it was better than just getting rent.' The highly successful Barry Burnett Organization is now located in the offices of the Prince of Wales Theatre and the landlord is Cameron Mackintosh.

Financially, Ariadne was living very close to the edge. 'Most Thursdays we had to pawn Robin's wife's jewellery in St Martin's Lane so we could pay the actors on the Friday and then pay her back with the cheque that came on Saturday from the theatre. Then she would reclaim the jewellery on the Monday, and hope that people asked her out to dinner on only Tuesdays and Wednesdays.'

Then, after Ariadne had proved to be the goddess of dodgy tours, Cameron formed a new company with one of the last of the actor–managers (and an undischarged bankrupt), Patrick Desmond, who advised him that the only way up was on the rapidly ageing back of old Agatha Christie thrillers. 'Our touring production of *Murder at the Vicarage* was legendary, not least because the legs of our stage manager were precisely the same shape as those of the table, so that when she got up from behind it we all used to think the table was moving. If people got fed up with *Murder at the Vicarage* we used to move the french windows from stage left to stage right, put a new cover on the sofa, call it *Black Coffee*, and bill the fortnight as a Festival of Christie. In those days you could go to the Nuffield in Southampton and speak to nice George Batty, who ran their wonderful scenery store. You'd take whatever you wanted, a pair of french windows, a couple of doors, whack it all together with some old curtains, and there was your set. At the end of the first week, you'd give the Nuffield £100 and the promise of future rentals and you were off and running. The other thing Pat taught me was that if we opened bank accounts in far-flung places like Jersey and Aberdeen, it would

Cameron picking a pocket or two from Lionel Bart, the composer of *Oliver!*, whose show set up Cameron's career and with whom he has sustained a thirty-year close friendship.

take our cheques that much longer to clear, and that way we could buy ourselves three or four more days of box-office income before they started to bounce.'

At this time, the very beginning of his producing career, Cameron learned all the lessons he would need to survive in the shaky and chaotic world of the commercial theatre. He also learned how to graft. 'We were the publi-cists as well as the producers, the company managers and the accountants, and it was very hard work, especially as one of us always had to stay a week ahead of the tour to drum up trade. It was no good having a full house on a Saturday night in one town if you opened to nobody on the Monday in the next. We couldn't afford to hire anyone except the cast, so Pat and I were really living off our wits.'

NEW THEATRE — KINGSTON UPON HULL
PHONE 20463

Props.: Kingston upon Hull New Theatre Co. Ltd.   Administrator & Licensee: William Sharpe, T.M.A.

Week commencing MONDAY, JANUARY 31st, 1972

MONDAY to FRIDAY at 7.30   SATURDAY at 5 and 8   MATINEE: THURSDAY at 2.30

CAMERON MACKINTOSH for Piccadilly Plays Ltd
and HARROGATE THEATRE present

The Enchanting Magical Musical!

SALAD DAYS

Book & Lyrics by
DOROTHY REYNOLDS · JULIAN SLADE

Music by
JULIAN SLADE

Musical Numbers Staged by
MALCOLM CLARE

Sets & Costumes by **ANDREW & MARGARET BROWNFOOT** · Musical Director **ALAN LEIGH**

Directed by **BRIAN HOWARD**

Production Advisor **JULIAN SLADE**

Cameron and his beloved magic piano go on the road.

3

A GLIMPSE OF STOCKING AND MRS DALE

"Heaven knows, anything goes"

'First of all, no matter how many great songs there are in a score, it is no good unless you get the book right'

By now, early in 1969, Cameron was scraping a living with various terrible tours and working out of Patrick Desmond's front room in Lamb's Conduit Street, Bloomsbury, having himself no office nor even a telephone.

But he still couldn't resist the lure of musicals: 'I had fallen in love with a record (borrowed from the library because I couldn't afford to buy it) of Cole Porter's 1934 *Anything Goes*, which had not at that time had a major post-war British revival, and it seemed to me to have the potential to give me my first really big hit.' His first problem was to raise the money and here, once again, his family proved unusually supportive. His father, Ian, had a seemingly well-heeled friend with a grand flat in Knightsbridge, and Cameron also scrounged

some initial money from Decca Records. His plan was to do it small at the Yvonne Arnaud Theatre in Guildford, then run a brief tour, and finally come in to a similarly modest West End theatre. The plan went wrong in just about every possible way. 'A week before rehearsals the backer turned out to have no money. I then had to go back to get more funding from Decca and beg a few other bits and pieces just to keep the show in rehearsal. David Dean who originally invested £250, finally invested £12,000. The show was quite a success in the intimacy of Guildford, but then we found that theatres on the road were much bigger and really needed an altogether expanded production. By the time I had finished the tour I was still scrabbling for more backers, the leading lady had left, as had the director and musical direc-

1969 – Cameron up West at last, now twenty-three and solo for the first time. A revival of Cole Porter's *Anything Goes* didn't; it opened at Guildford, staggered through a catastrophic tour, and finished up at the Saville where it limped along just long enough to lose Cameron every penny he and his friends had invested.

tor. At that point, if I had known anything about musicals, that is when I would – and should – have pulled the plug. But inexperienced as I was, I assumed that musicals were always like this and went blithely ahead with my London plans, even though the only theatre vacant was the 1500-seat Saville (now the ABC Shaftesbury Avenue) which was about three times the scale of the show we had originally planned for the Duke of York's, which had backed out at the last minute.'

Reviews were catastrophic for the production and its eventual star, the jazz singer Marion Montgomery, and *Anything Goes* survived barely twenty performances. 'I ended up quite literally in the dark, staring out at the vast barren wastes of an empty Saville Theatre. We closed on the second Saturday and that night Richard Mills [then Bernard Delfont's producing partner who ran the Saville, and later Mackintosh's executive in running the Prince Edward and the Prince of Wales] came up to me in the empty stalls bar and said, "I know you are utterly heartbroken, but I'll tell you one thing. If you survive this, you'll survive in our business. And," he added, "I said exactly the same words, in exactly the same place, to Bernie Delfont twenty-five years ago."'

Cameron was not easily to forget the lessons of *Anything Goes*: 'First of all, no matter how many great songs there are in a score it is no good unless you get the book right, and on this occasion the book was fatally dated. Second, I learned the importance of matching the right show to the right theatre. Then again, I lost £45,000 of the bank's and other people's money, which for 1969 was a very great deal. I made hundreds of mistakes, but I did learn my

very first lesson about the importance of book structure in any musical, and that I've never forgotten. But it still didn't put me off as a producer, because I kept thinking this was the musical norm.'

Luckily Richard Mills was to be proven right, though at that moment there was precious little justification for his cool optimism. Cameron had lost nearly all his backers and had also lost face by coming into the wrong West End theatre with a major flop; worst of all, he temporarily lost faith in himself. For at least a week.

Back in the office Barry was somewhat surprised to find that Cameron chose this moment to hire his first staff member. It was six months before he admitted, somewhat sheepishly, that the efficient professional secretary he had engaged was in fact his mother, Diana, who in various domestic and other ways was in reality still keeping him, convinced as always that it was only a matter of time before her boy came good. His confidence duly returned, and she tells of the limousines he hired to take them to first nights and the champagne and flowers ordered for friends and colleagues. Not for a moment did he let anyone in the business know how much the failure of *Anything Goes* had hurt him, and in presenting his confident face to the world, Diana was his greatest ally.

Although his heart was still in musicals, even Cameron had now learned that, if there was still no business like showbusiness, there might yet be cheaper ways of establishing himself as an impresario. The venerable character actor Charles Simon had been for several decades playing Dr Dale in the highest-rated of all BBC radio pioneering soap operas, *Mrs Dale's Diary*, and he had used some of his spare studio time

to weave the much-loved characters into a stage play. One of Cameron's few remaining backers, the Hon. George Borwick (heir to the baking powder) who was in partnership with Martin Tickner, gave him the rights for a modest and, it turned out, worthless interest. Accordingly he picked up a straight play, and one that seemed to have considerable potential.

This was to be directed by another theatrical figure of distinction, the Australian Allan Davis, and for a while at least it looked as though nothing could go wrong with a brisk tour. They duly opened under Cameron's sole management at the Ashcroft Theatre, Croydon, at the start of what was intended to be a thirty-

week tour, the longest and most ambitious that the tyro producer had ever undertaken.

'It rapidly became horribly clear to me that the only people booking this tour were theatre managers who made the same mistake we had. The public stayed away in their thousands. The third date of the tour was to be a fortnight at the Winter Gardens in Blackpool which, even out of season, was a great date with 2,500 seats. Nobody came, and I do mean nobody. On the first night we took ten shillings. By the end of the first week we had taken £220, and by the end of the second £250; "Cheer up Mr Mackintosh," said the house manager, "at least it's building."'

(From left to right) Marion Montgomery, Bernard Sharpe and Janet Mahoney in *Anything Goes*.

Right – A few years later, managing a tour of *Hair*, Cameron comes up with an even more exotic marketing ploy, and this one in English. The 'Hair Rail' scheme involved going to your nearest railway station and booking a combined theatre and rail ticket for a mere twenty-four shillings. Surprisingly few did, possibly believing that if British Rail were still unable to get the trains running on time, their chances of getting an entire show on schedule were also somewhat remote.

What Mackintosh had failed to understand, and in all fairness it has been a mistake made by older and wiser managers over the years, is that the theatregoing public has never shown any desire to see its favourite radio characters brought to life on the stage, precisely because they have already imagined them in their minds' eyes while listening to the wireless and have no wish to be disillusioned by a confrontation with an actor looking nothing like the character they have visualized. Only six weeks into this cataclysmic tour even the longest-suffering of his bank managers faced with Cameron's problems had to make a choice; Cameron could either declare bankruptcy, in which case none of the actors would get paid and he would be banned by Equity from further productions, or they could give him an utterly unsecured loan of £500 to pay off the cast. They chose the latter and the show closed, but this unusual act of faith proved to be Cameron's salvation. He is also, ironically, now one of that bank's most valued clients.

In those considerably more gentle theatrical days, none of the other theatres due for the production demanded penalty payments, and Mackintosh lived to fight another day, though for now it was clear even to him that he would have, for the moment at least, to shelve any other plans he might cherish about remaining in management. Instead, he went off to Glasgow and joined the tour of *Hair* as publicity manager, a show he stayed with in Scotland for the next eighteen months, looking after and devising wild publicity schemes for both the Scottish and national tour. This was Cameron's first stab at marketing, at which he was later to excel. One of his most ingenious wheezes was his 'Hair Rail' scheme, whereby members of the public could buy their theatre tickets along with their train tickets at their local station.

Although modestly salaried, and no longer increasing his considerable overdraft, Cameron never made any secret of his determination to go back to being a producer. His earlier experiences on the road and at the Saville had in no way discouraged this ambition, and the show he took on to kick-start his producing career was the one that had started it all, *Salad Days*.

Unusually in his business, Cameron has always been immensely sentimental and loving about those who have in any way helped him in the past, so, early in the autumn of 1971, he decided it was time to pay tribute to Julian Slade and the magic piano that had started his lifelong fascination with stage musicals. He therefore revived *Salad Days* on the road, with his brother Robert playing piano in the pit, and then, to indicate his continuing belief in the future of the British musical in general, and Julian Slade in particular, decided to stage Slade's latest score. This he did in partnership with another great friend of Julian's, Veronica Flint-Shipman, who with her husband owned and ran the Phoenix Theatre for many years; both were also to become members of Cameron's inner circle of lifelong friends.

Their first production together was *Trelawny*, a lyrical and enchanting musical version of one of the greatest of backstage romantic dramas,

33

Pinero's 1898 *Trelawny of the Wells*, and it reopened the handsomely refurbished Bristol Old Vic, home of the original *Salad Days* and other Slade hits of the 1950s. Cameron and Veronica took it out from the Bristol Old Vic and brought it first to Sadler's Wells, the show's setting, and then to the Prince of Wales. Gemma Craven made her West End debut in the title role, and as her boyfriend's irate Victorian papa, determined not to let his beloved son (Ian Richardson in his musical debut) get mixed up with theatrical trash, Max Adrian made what was sadly to be his last appearance: he died during the run. In London, *Trelawny* achieved a thoroughly respectable 177 performances and could, in that light, be considered Cameron's first real hit.

Despite generally good and supportive reviews, the musical played to an average of only 60 per cent, and barely recouped any of its capital and therefore could not afford to make another transfer. All the same, *Trelawny* had got Cameron off the road and back into the heart of the West End, and with a musical at that. It was there he now intended to stay.

When Cameron was twenty-six he saw his first Broadway show with its original cast intact. It was to change his life. Stephen Sondheim's *Company* opened in January 1972 and

Veronica Flint-Shipman & Cameron Mackintosh present THE BRISTOL OLD VIC production

TRELAWNY

IAN RICHARDSON and MAX ADRIAN

and producers

GEMMA CRAVEN as TRELAWNY

Book by AUBREY WOODS · Music & Lyrics by JULIAN SLADE with

TEDDY GREEN · ELIZABETH POWER · DAVID MORTON
JOHN GOWER · BETTY BENFIELD · JOHN WATTS
VERONICA CLIFFORD · ROY SKELTON
AND

JOYCE CAREY   Directed by VAL MAY

A MARVELLOUS MUSICAL!

Sadler's Wells Theatre
ROSEBERY AVENUE LONDON E.C.1 Tel 01-837 1672

Arriving (above) at the gala charity production of the Victorian musical "Trelawny" at Sadler's Wells Theatre, Finsbury, in true Victorian style on Monday are (from left to right) co-producers *Cameron Mackintosh* and Veronica Flint-Shipman, Mr Gerald Flint-Shipman and Mrs Diana Mackintosh, *Cameron's* mother.

Cameron was, as he said, 'beside myself because I couldn't yet afford to go to America so I fought my way to an opening night ticket and, absolutely hysterical, stood and cheered.'

Living by now in a Soho bedsit, he made himself a familiar figure around the bars and restaurants of Theatreland and a habitué of Shaftesbury Avenue, where he met the next major contributor to his production aspirations. Michael Codron was then, and is still, the most influential and intelligent commercial manager of the West End, but one with limited interest in the afterlife of his shows. He and Cameron were therefore the perfect match, in that they agreed that Mackintosh would take on Codron's early Ayckbourn and Simon Gray hits as they left the West End, giving them some extra weeks on the road with strong television players like James Bolam in leading roles.

Nearly respectable, not only for the

1972 – Julian Slade, Cameron's first mentor, returns to his magic piano for a lyrical and enchanting musical version of Pinero's *Trelawny of the Wells*, which triumphantly reopened the Bristol Old Vic. It did not fare as well in London, despite the trouble taken by Cameron (below left), his mother, Diana, and his co-producers, Gerald and Veronica Flint-Shipman, to arrive at the gala at Sadler's Wells first night in suitably period costume.

WYVERN THEATRE, SW

CIVIC CENTRE Box Office: APRIL 2nd

Jame[s]

Bu[

"A very fine & very funny evening"

calibre of his touring work but also because of his new-found ability actually to pay his cast and even himself on Saturday nights with non-bouncing cheques, Mackintosh now turned his mind back towards the musicals that had always been, and were always to remain, his chief theatrical love. Indeed from now on he was almost never again to get involved with anything that didn't have at least one piano on the stage or in the pit.

King of the Road – Throughout the early 1970s Cameron survived as a touring manager, largely by producing recent West End hits as quickly and economically as his still-limited budget would allow. He was learning the business that was later to lie at the heart of his empire – getting the show on the road and keeping it there as long as possible. At this time, his co-producers would include family, friends and anyone with a few bob to spare; sets were recycled as often as the shows and on one memorable occasion, his co-producers were the Bristol Rovers Football Club.

Another lesson had been learned: take the money where you find it and try to pay it back as slowly as possible.

The Card, across twenty years. Arnold Bennett's classic novel of the likely lad, Denry Machin, first starred Jim Dale (above). It was effectively the show that took him to West End and Broadway stardom as a leading man in musicals.

4

FROM SLADE TO SONDHEIM

‘Making a new tomorrow’

‘I've never believed the theory that a producer shouldn't "meddle" with what is happening on his stage’

Soon after *Trelawny*, Cameron embarked on what would develop slowly but surely into his first original musical. He went back to the Bristol Old Vic, but now on very different terms; whereas he had simply 'picked up' *Trelawny* from there, made a few very minor alterations and taken it on the road, this new show was to have his imprint on it long before rehearsals even began.

Some years earlier, he had fallen in love with the Alec Guinness 1940s film version of *The Card*, Arnold Bennett's original and classic novel. Like all the great fairy-tales from *Cinderella* to *My Fair Lady* (with which Cameron was soon to be much involved), this was the story of someone going to a ball. In this case it is Denry Machin, the 'card' of Bennett's title, and the story of his making good became in Cameron's hands one of the most joyous, engaging and energetic British stage musicals since Tommy Steele's *Half A Sixpence*.

Both stories came from bestsellers of the early part of the century, and both had the theme of a likely lad hero who overcomes rigid class oppression to turn the tables on his stiff Victorian elders and betters. Denry is a lovable kind of pioneer yuppie; his morals may be a little shaky, his methods a little suspect, but precisely because he is in there fighting for a future among people who have only a past, we side with his determination to overturn a century of snobbery with violence.

On this occasion Mackintosh recalled two relatively new friends, the then husband-and-wife musical team of Tony Hatch and Jackie Trent. Jackie came from Bennett's Staffordshire Potteries. Having signed them up, he approached two other North Country writers

The original production of *The Card* in 1973 was joined by Dinah Sheridan when Eleanor Bron left the cast. The show was then to reappear twenty years later in very different productions at the Watermill in Newbury and at the Open Air Theatre in Regents Park, with costume designs by Tim Goodchild.

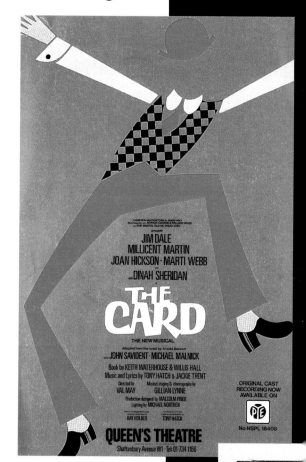

CAMERON MACKINTOSH & JERRY NICK
presents AN ARNOLD CLAYTON & WILLIAM WOOD
of THE BRISTOL OLD VIC TRUST LTD'S

JIM DALE
MILLICENT MARTIN
JOAN HICKSON · MARTI WEBB
with DINAH SHERIDAN

THE CARD
THE NEW MUSICAL

Adapted from the novel by Arnold Bennett
with JOHN SAVIDENT · MICHAEL MALNICK
Book by KEITH WATERHOUSE & WILLIS HALL
Music and Lyrics by TONY HATCH & JACKIE TRENT
Directed by   Musical staging & choreography by
VAL MAY   GILLIAN LYNNE
Production designed by MALCOLM PRIDE
Lighting by MICHAEL NORTHEN

RAY HOLDER   TONY HATCH

QUEEN'S THEATRE
Shaftesbury Avenue W1 · Tel: 01-734 1166

ORIGINAL CAST
RECORDING NOW
AVAILABLE ON
PYE
No NSPL 18408

famous for their understanding of the period, Keith Waterhouse and Willis Hall, and set the whole team together with Gillian Lynne as choreographer and Val May, the director of *Trelawny*, now director of the Bristol Old Vic, in overall charge.

'I've never believed the theory that a producer shouldn't "meddle" with what is happening on his stage; *Trelawny* happened to be in a very good state when I got to it, so all I did there was suggest that Julian might like to alter one of his ballads, which he did. But the idea of doing *The Card* as a musical started with me, because I had always loved the Alec Guinness film, and once there was a treatment from Waterhouse and Hall, we all had meetings at

which I threw in my two pennyworth; I got very involved with the structure, although we never really got that right in the second half, I think perhaps because the relentlessness of Denry's success at climbing the social ladder meant there was never going to be enough real conflict.'

One of the most crucial talents for any producer is the ability to bring the right people together at the right time on the right project, and Cameron's instincts have very seldom let him down. Although still unable to finance the show out of his own pocket, Cameron discovered that H. M. Tennent's new American owner (following the death of Binkie Beaumont), Arthur Cantor, was in London. Cameron went to his hotel armed with a silver tongue and a demo tape, played him a single song, and Cantor agreed on the spot to raise most of the money.

With a strong cast headed by Jim Dale, Millicent Martin, Joan Hickson, Eleanor Bron and Marti Webb, *The Card* opened at the Bristol Old Vic early in 1973, transferred from there to the West End and survived a respectable 130 performances. Yet despite reviews which were in the main very enthusiastic, it lacked that indefinable magic which could transform a good show into a smash hit. Cameron's investors barely got their money back, and while most producers would simply have drawn a line under the experience, he is not most producers.

WATERMILL
theatre & restaurant

THE CARD

23 JULY – 5 SEPTEMBER

SPONSORED BY TARMAC CONSTRUCTION

Twenty years on, in 1992, when he was already the most successful West End and Broadway producer in the world, Jill Fraser at the Watermill Theatre in Newbury (who was on the same Central School stage management course as Cameron in 1964) wanted to revive *The Card*. Cameron agreed, subject to a reworking of the script, and a year later arranged for it to be mounted at the Open Air Theatre in Regent's Park and subsequently toured it, amazingly as far as Moscow. It is good to think that Denry Machin, the wide-boy of the Potteries, can therefore claim considerable responsibility for the triumph of *glasnost*. Even though his financial involvement was then minimal, and there was no real chance of a return to the West End, Cameron was calling meetings with the creative team to fine-tune a show he still regards as a work in progress.

But back then, in 1973, the time had come for him to regroup and reconsider; neither *The Card* nor *Trelawny* could have been termed outright failures, but neither were they the kind of money-making hits to inspire confidence from his backers or even in himself. The most that could really have been said about them was that they had survived for a few months in an already expensive West End climate.

'What I learned from those shows was that I actually hadn't learned enough; I still didn't know what really made a musical succeed or fail on its own terms, and I knew that in the immediate future I only wanted to work on shows that were already well written, so I could learn my craft.'

There were those who thought he already knew plenty. Arthur Cantor, despite having lost money on *The Card*, brought him *Godspell*, a

show that Cameron had adored during its original London run at the then trendy fringe converted engine shed, the Round House.

'I took over the secondary touring rights of *Godspell*, and stayed with that score for almost all of the rest of the 1970s, taking it up and down the country and into about seven London theatres for brief return engagements. It was a magnificent learning experience, working in a sort of playschool with almost a dozen actors who were forever playing identity games to keep the show fresh; it was the first ensemble I'd ever worked in, and without my realizing it, it set the artistic seed for working on another ensemble musical in the 1980s – *Les*

Rocking through the 1970s – Where *Godspell* proved one of Cameron's best little earners on the road, the all-too-similar *Rock Nativity* (right) died a deservedly rapid death. Above – The roadshow of *Godspell*, notable for a semi-nude David Burt (centre) and a characteristically restrained Su Pollard (second left), while (on the far right) is the future

General Secretary of the Arts Council and, very briefly, General Director of Covent Garden, Mary Allen. When the show reached Her Majesty's in May 1977, Harry Secombe joined a cast party that included his son, Andrew, (back left) and (next to him) a young Paul Kerryson, who later directed many great Sondheim revivals around the country.

Misérables. I found a very strong team of performers at the very start of their careers, and in a sense *Godspell* was my very first hit in that we ran it for about five and a half years, popping back into the West End whenever a theatre fell temporarily vacant and they wanted something cheap and cheerful and paid me a much-needed guarantee to cover my costs.'

The key to the success Cameron had all over the place with *Godspell* was that he now knew more than any other young manager about the ins and outs of small-scale touring: which theatres were good for which shows, which were the ones to avoid, which were the best for getting your money out fast and not having too

many backstage troubles with the set. It was, and remains, a specialist art, often ignored by producers interested only in the bright lights of the big city, but a detailed knowledge of touring, in these years at home and then later worldwide, is still at the very heart of the Mackintosh operation.

For now, so struck was he by the possibilities of the rock gospel after *Godspell* that he tried to build another one, *Rock Nativity*, which eventually opened at Newcastle in February 1976 with a cast headed by Helen Chapelle. Again, Cameron brought some old friends together for it; he had been touring some David Wood children's musical plays such as *The Owl and the Pussycat* and *The Gingerbread Man* and persuaded him to write the book, for which Tony Hatch and Jackie Trent of *The Card* would compose the score.

'We all worked very hard on that one, but somehow it always seemed to lurch between *Jesus Christ Superstar* and *Joseph and the Amazing Technicolour Dreamcoat*, without ever being as good as either. In a desperate attempt to improve business on the last week of the tour, by which time we had got to Wimbledon, I changed the title to *Make a New Tomorrow* but the show patently failed to do that either, and we closed it without ever coming any closer than that to the West End.'

So these years back on the road were by no means always triumphant; the only difference now was that he always had *Godspell* to underpin and finance tours that were markedly less successful. Another of these was *Lauder* in 1976, a musical biography of Sir Harry done as a one-man show by the great Scots comedian Jimmy Logan, at his most kilted. It was the first of Cameron's shows to go on a world tour, playing to expatriate Scots.

'Though it didn't make any money, Jimmy was wonderful in it; I've always been devoted to Scotland, have kept a home there for many years, and remember having to make fleeting appearances in Glasgow in *Hair*; on the last night, eager Scots audiences could have caught a glimpse of me in the nude scene, though that was almost my last professional appearance on any stage. I think the thought of showing myself naked to several hundred total strangers was what finally put me off any kind of public life in the theatre.'

Far from being inactive in the mid-seventies, it nevertheless seemed that Cameron was marking time, waiting for something that, like *The Card*, he could turn from an idea into (at the least) a respectable run, but he was unwilling to chance his arm or raid his now-limited backers again until the right project came along. In the meantime he chose some low-key and generally safe bets: short Christmas seasons of such children's plays as Julian Slade's *Winnie the Pooh* and David Wood's *The Owl and the Pussycat*, a tour of *The Rocky Horror Show* (in Britain and in Germany, years before it was fashionable or financially rewarding), another David Wood (*The Gingerbread Man*) and of course the everlasting, ever-profitable *Godspell*.

Coasting now, when his next big hit did come along he very nearly missed it altogether. In 1976 two neighbouring theatres in the Strand were housing long runs: the Vaudeville

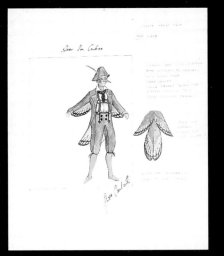

Theatre for children – A
strong alliance with the
writer David Wood led to
such long-running hits as
The Gingerbread Man
(Clive Dunn as Herr von
Cuckoo), *The Owl and
the Pussycat* (Verity Anne
Meldrum and Gordon
Griffin) and Julian
Slade's *Winnie the Pooh*
(Christopher Biggins as
Pooh, David Glover as
Eeyore and Chris Melville
as Piglet). If you want an
audience of adults, you
had better start by
catching them young.

'*I cannot think of a more boring evening, unless it be a reading of the* Book of Kells'
— *Stephen Sondheim on* Side by Side

had Alan Ayckbourn's *The Norman Conquests*, with Julia McKenzie and Millicent Martin, while next door at the Adelphi, David Kernan and Jean Simmons were in the London pre-mière of Stephen Sondheim's whipped-cream-with-knives adaptation of an Ingmar Bergman movie, *A Little Night Music*. The two compa-nies would meet every week for tea on matinee days, and at one of these Kernan announced that he had been asked by Cleo Laine, at her Wavendon Festival Theatre up the M1, to put together an evening of Sondheim songs chosen from the half-dozen or so scores he had by then written. If Millie and Julia agreed, they and Kernan would do most of the singing, and Ned Sherrin would write and narrate the con-cert. From that one-night start, the little show began growing, changing and ultimately devel-oping into *Side by Side by Sondheim*, and it wasn't long before the company believed they were on to something which might have a full commercial life in the West End. Nobody was more surprised by this than Sondheim himself: 'I cannot think,' he wrote to Kernan in a letter giving him permission to go ahead, 'of a more boring evening, unless it be a reading of the *Book of Kells*.'

For a while at least it seemed that most man-agements agreed; the concept of the 'book and stool show' as it was christened by Caryl Brahms, Sherrin's long-time collaborator on this and many other more orthodox musicals and plays, was still not widely appreciated, and although Sondheim already had a limited cult following, he had not yet achieved the almost religious worship he enjoys worldwide today. Three singers, two pianists, one narrator and nothing but random songs which often made

little sense outside the scores for which they were first written? Managements were not exactly lined up waving fistfuls of five-pound notes for options, but the show had done well enough for one night at Wavendon to ensure a return visit a few months later, and this time Kernan and Sherrin persuaded Cameron at least to have a look. Mackintosh is not how-ever the most organized of drivers, and his sense of direction is legendarily awful. In search of Wavendon this Sunday night he set off on the motorway from London, only to dis-cover from a friendly local policeman, after about an hour and a half, that he had been dri-ving down the M4 whereas Wavendon is in fact situated up the M1.

Moreover he was due the next day in New York, so his chances of ever seeing the show seemed slight as *Side by Side by Sondheim* only had one more scheduled engagement – yet another one-night stand, this time in an old hospital operating theatre, which had been

Cameron goes global – After a lengthy British tour, his production of Richard O'Brien's camp cult horror movie musical *The Rocky Horror Show* takes Berlin by storm. Frank N. Furter (played by the author) finally got down among the Frankfurters.

1976 – 'Isn't it warm, isn't it rosy?' Cameron's first West End hit was a joyous anthology of the songs of Stephen Sondheim. Narrated by Ned Sherrin (and subsequently Robin Ray, Hermione Gingold, Sheridan Morley and Michael Parkinson among many others), it starred (left to right) Julia McKenzie, David Kernan and Millicent Martin. It ran for nearly two years in the West End, plus another whole season on Broadway, followed by long road tours and frequent revivals through the 1980s and 1990s.

converted into the Greenwood Theatre and is now a south London television studio. Feeling somewhat sheepish about having taken the wrong motorway, Mackintosh persuaded some great friends, George Borwick, Barry Burnett and the actor and *Pooh* star Christopher Biggins, to go and see the show at the Greenwood and phone him in New York if they really thought it had a future.

Borwick and Biggins hit the transatlantic phone as soon as they left the theatre, reporting ecstatically on the musical and its reception, and there and then Cameron bought the transfer rights, in partnership with the Aus-tralian manager Helen Montagu, on behalf of H. M. Tennent. By now they were about the only two West End producers who had not somewhere seen the show. All the others had regretfully declined it on the grounds that only theatre buffs would like it and it would undoubtedly close in preview.

It took *Side by Side by Sondheim* several more months to reach the stages of first the Mermaid, then Wyndham's and finally the Garrick. When it did, the critics loved it and so did the audiences. It proved to be the most enduring of Cameron's early shows and continues to be produced in many countries and languages.

WYNDHAM'S
Charing Cross Road WC2 **THEATRE** Telephone 01-836 3028

"A SCINTILLATING NEW HIT"
"THE AUDIENCE JUST WENT WILD"
"DAZZLING" "A TRIUMPH"
SIDE BY SIDE BY SONDHEIM

"AN EXCITING MUSICAL ENTERTAINMENT"

**MILLICENT MARTIN
JULIA McKENZIE
DAVID KERNAN
NED SHERRIN**

STEPHEN SONDHEIM

NED SHERRIN   RAY COOK   BOB HOWE   TIM HIGGS & STUART PEDLAR   PETER DOCHERTY
GINA FRATINI   JOHN WOOD

RCA

It was also the first show to introduce Sondheim to the mass British audience.

It has now achieved classic status. A year later it became the first of the Mackintosh shows to hit New York, transferring with its original cast to Broadway, where it ran another year, but not under Cameron Mackintosh's own management. In fact, Sondheim, having reserved the US rights for his then producer Harold Prince, opened it under his banner and Cameron wasn't even invited to the opening night. Then it went out on a British national tour during which Sherrin was replaced first by Cyril Ritchard, who died during the run and then by Hermione Gingold.

At home the show ran on in London and on the road, where there have been a long line of narrators starting with Robin Ray and Russell Harty and subsequently including such varied talents as those of Michael Parkinson, Bernard

Braden, Michael Aspel, Christopher Biggins and Sheridan Morley. This was also, of course, the start of a long personal and professional association between Sondheim and Mackintosh leading eventually to the London *Follies* of 1987 which ran for two years (twice the Broadway original), by which time Sondheim had been officially welcomed as the greatest living Broadway composer.

Once again, having got involved with a show, Cameron was determined never to let it go; twenty years after the original triumphant West End opening of *Side by Side,* Mackintosh had bought up all the rights in it from the original cast (who had formed themselves into the InComes Company in salute to one of the best title songs even Sondheim ever wrote) and licensed it for regional performances even while embarking on its successor, *Putting it Together,* which deals with the second half of Sondheim's scores. *Putting it Together* was directed by Julia McKenzie and starred Julie Andrews, lured back to off-Broadway in 1994 by Cameron and Julia, after a twenty-five-year absence.

But at the time of that first *Side by Side,* perceptions were very different, as Kurt Ganzl noted: 'With *Side by Side,* Britain, which had only ever given Sondheim's works limited appreciation, suddenly discovered the wit and wonder of his words and music in an evening which displayed the numbers naked, without the often irritating characters who had originally delivered them in their various plays. The entertainment was a major London success, and its pocket size helped it to be toured and produced throughout the country in regional theatres, spreading the composer's work far and wide in a way that London productions of *A Funny Thing Happened on the Way to the Forum* or *Company* or latterly *Gypsy* had not done. With *Side by Side,* Britain suddenly woke up to the works of Sondheim and the little show then went on to Broadway and the English-speaking world, continuing its missionary work and creating happy zealots wherever it went.'

Not for the first time, and certainly not for the last, Mackintosh had been instrumental in the success of a show which was to change all perceptions of the musical theatre on both sides of the Atlantic. *Side by Side* did something still even more rare for Cameron at this time: it actually made him some money, as well as retaining his name above the title of a West End show for more than two years. With one small revue, albeit one of remarkable endurance over the years, Cameron Mackintosh had at last achieved full respectability as a West End producer.

If only showbiz success were always that easy. Suddenly, thanks largely to his touring success and *Side by Side by Sondheim*, Mackintosh had within a few months become the most respected young producer around Shaftesbury Avenue. That distinction brought him the dubious honour of being asked to produce the annual awards ceremony for the Society of West End Theatre, one at which he proposed the highlight should be Elaine Paige singing 'Don't Cry For Me Argentina' since *Evita* had won Best Musical of the Year.

Cameron, faced with building a tightly-timed running order for the television coverage, reckoned that one girl, one mike, one song, would be the safest option; but *Evita's* composer, Andrew Lloyd Webber, whom Cameron had never met, took the view that a rather longer medley of the show's hit numbers, requiring numerous complicated technical mike changes, would be a better idea. Lloyd Webber won that argument, but on the night most of the sound system collapsed and therefore *Evita* didn't sound precisely as Andrew Lloyd Webber had intended. Its now-irate composer decided that Mackintosh was to blame, and claimed in his acceptance speech that the

breakdown would never have occurred if 'a real producer like Hal Prince' had been in charge. After the dinner that followed Cameron, reinforced by an entire bottle of claret, tried to find Andrew in order to break the empty bottle over his head. Luckily for the future of the British musical theatre, David Land (who had discovered Rice and Lloyd Webber) found Cameron first. The judicious application of yet another drink had Mackintosh under the table, thereby avoiding a confrontation that could have made the two men enemies.

A few days later Andrew Lloyd Webber wrote a contrite note of apology. Cameron, with typical grace, accepted his apology and, as far as he was concerned, it was over. Their meeting, which they couldn't possibly have believed would have such significant and hugely fortunate consequences, would not take place for another three years.

1977 – '*After Shave* was my last real bona fide flop.' It ran very briefly in the West End and had the dubious distinction of not just closing 1979 but also of closing the entire genre of revue.

Cameron Mackintosh presents

After Shave

A MUSICAL REVUE

Cameron Mackintosh presents
AFTER SHAVE
Written by
STEPHEN WYATT
Music Composed by
NIC ROWLEY
with
SUE ALDRED
LINDA DOBELL
NICOLETTE MARVIN
CAROLINE NOH
BELINDA SINCLAIR
Directed and Choreographed by
CHRISTIE DICKASON
Musical Direction and Arrangements by NIC ROWLEY
Production Designed by CLIVE LAVAGNA
Sound by MALCOLM BLACKMOOR   Lighting by BRIAN HARRIS
Musical Associate PETER MOSS
the band
NIC ROWLEY Keyboards PETER MOSS Guitar Keyboards
DOUGIE HENNING Bass WILL HILL Percussion

APOLLO
THEATRE
Shaftesbury Avenue W1 Tel:01-437 2663

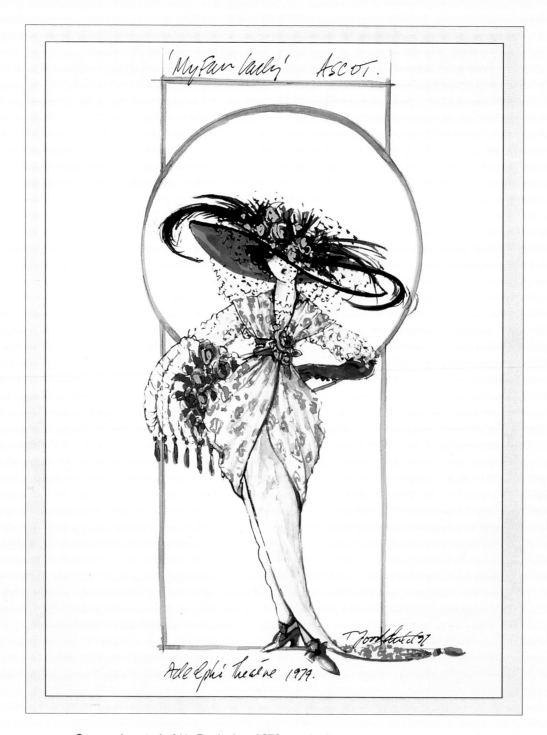

'My Fair Lady' ASCOT.

Adelphi Theatre 1979.

Cameron's revival of *My Fair Lady* in 1979 was the first ever to abandon the original Cecil Beaton costumes. An entirely new production was designed by Tim Goodchild.

5

TOUR DE FORCE AND FORCED TO TOUR

"I could have danced all night"

'My goal has never really changed: to try and do the best shows I can'

With the run of *Side by Side by Sondheim* happily continuing at the Garrick, Cameron started on what he had always loved best: a cycle of great and well-loved musicals built for the road but also capable of long West End revival runs. 'Even I had begun to realize that to try and produce two major original musicals (*Trelawny* and *The Card*) before I was twenty-five had been, to say the least, a little fool-hardy, and I had now had plenty of time to think about why they hadn't altogether worked, at least in commercial, profit-making terms. All the reverses I've ever had in my professional life have been good for me, in that they have made me close one door and open another. My goal has never really changed: to try and do the best shows I can. But the more shows I did at this time, the more I learned of the difficulties inherent in getting them just right. It all takes time, money and patience, and you have to make sure that you have enough of both before you start: it's no use getting on a treadmill of show after show, as that way you never get the time to stand back and look at what you are doing wrong.'

He now made no secret of his major ambition: a revival of his beloved *Oliver!*, the show which had given him his professional start as an assistant stage manager and which he still thinks of as the crucible of the modern musical. 'We were able to get the original Sean Kenny set out of mothballs, and even all the costumes; I found my own name still sewn into one of the Londoners' jackets. That set had always been the key to the show's initial success: using just a turntable and some trucks you can move *Oliver!* along so fast that the audience never has time to think about how it is being done. You are totally pulled into another world, and taught the language of the evening, and taken on the start of a journey; that's what I've come to demand of all my shows. It all stems from *Oliver!* The sets have to dance with the action. Sean Kenny's stark, stylized, Dickensian timbers are so choreographed that as you are taken from scene to scene you are unaware that you are seeing actors on moving trucks.'

In 1977, however, in the West End where it had already played for about five years, there wasn't much interest in seeing the Bart classic back so soon. Instead, Cameron took it to Leicester, but with a difference: this was not to be yet another cut-price roadshow, but a full replica of the original, designed to tour major theatres, those that used to be known as 'number one dates'. And he planned to do it in a manner thoroughly unusual for the time – not apologetically or cheaply, but as if it were a brand new show on its way *into* town instead of *out* of it. Because of the time and money lavished on it, this Leicester production (starring Roy Hudd in a brilliant if underrated performance as Fagin) scored a tremendous success in every town it played.

As a result, the show's original producer, Donald Albery, suggested that Cameron might like to bring it back to London as a three-month filler when its original theatre, now called the Albery, fell unexpectedly vacant. That three-month run stretched to two and a half years, and by now there was considerable interest in the regional revolution that Cameron had wrought at Leicester: the opening of old shows in such spectacular new stagings that they

1979 – With a little bit of luck…In collaboration with the Arts Council, Cameron sets up a lavish touring revival of *My Fair Lady* with the veteran impresario Harold Fielding (bottom left) as his co-producer and Dame Anna Neagle (right) as Mrs Higgins, here some years later celebrating her eightieth birthday. The lyricist Alan Jay Lerner (top left) took over the production as it moved into London and soon married its star, Liz Robertson, who played Eliza to the Henry Higgins of Tony Britton.

could take on a whole new life of their own, maybe even ending up back in the West End.

Happily for Cameron, the success of his own first *Oliver!* also coincided with the moment when the two great regional theatre chains then still flourishing, Moss Empires and Howard and Wyndham, started to offload their properties on to local councils who were able to get government funding to refurbish and update premises, once the city-centre pride of the local community, which had threatened to become inner-city eyesores or at best bingo halls. There was still a problem, however, and one that is echoed at the time of this writing twenty years

later by the advent of the Lottery: council money was being made available for the restoration of these often late-nineteenth-century buildings, but no thought had been given as to where the shows to fill them with audiences might be found.

Because of the success of *Oliver!*, an enlightened Arts Council director, Tony Fields, had the brainwave of offering Cameron hard Arts Council cash to mount a major musical to tour and therefore fill the newly revitalized stages. There then followed a good deal of grumbling from those who felt that the classical remit of the Council was being vulgarized by putting its

money into a Broadway blockbuster, rather than the more traditional orchestra or chorus, opera or ballet.

To mute the protests, a characteristic compromise was reached – Cameron could have Arts Council funding for keeping major civic theatres around the country alive with the sound of old musicals, provided that a 'suitable' musical could be found. This sounds easier than it was. Cameron's first choice was *The Sound of Music*, which had never toured Britain, but Tony Fields didn't think even he

could get singing nuns on to an Arts Council agenda, which although in favour of revitalizing regional theatre still wished to do so in an at least faintly cultural fashion. The answer turned out to be a great Lerner–Loewe score, which at least had the saving grace of being based on Bernard Shaw's *Pygmalion*. It was, of course, *My Fair Lady*.

Given the go-ahead at last and several thousand Arts Council pounds, Cameron was determined to recapture the spirit of the original but with new visual designs and modern stage

Liz Robertson dreaming of a room somewhere, far away from the cold night air, at the start of Cameron's 1979 revival of *My Fair Lady*.

technology. With considerable help from Alan Jay Lerner, Cameron was now able to come up with a fresh production, which retained the original magic without becoming a museum piece, a trick he was to repeat with James Hammerstein in the subsequent revival of *Oklahoma!* 'We were the first production ever to abandon the Cecil Beaton sets and costumes and start again with an entirely new design by Tim Goodchild; I also brought in Gillian Lynne as the choreographer, Tony Britton as a very Shavian Higgins, Liz Robertson in her first starring role as Eliza, Peter Baylis as an irrepressible Dolittle and the original staging by Robin Midgeley at Leicester was taken over later by Alan Jay Lerner who then married Liz, giving the whole show a fairy-tale quality. But the problem was that the show had been done to death in the regions both by the amateurs and by the local repertory theatres. To give ourselves legitimacy I persuaded the great Dame Anna Neagle to join the cast as Mrs Higgins. There had never been, since the original, a production as lavish or carefully built and rehearsed and choreographed as ours. When we eventually came into London and opened at the Adelphi, the reviews were almost exactly as good as they had been the very first time around, and I am still very proud of that.'

What Mackintosh had established with this *My Fair Lady* (apart from the start of a crucially important alliance with Goodchild and Lynne) was, once again, something that would stay with him for the rest of his career; the simple but then still revolutionary idea that audiences outside the capital were entitled to productions every bit as expensive and expert as those who had been lucky enough to be there on the origi-

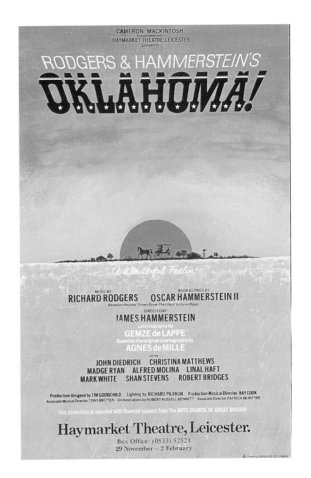

nal first nights, either in the West End or on Broadway. Distance no longer made the shows grow cheaper or lazier.

And what had worked once could surely be made to work again – no sooner was *My Fair Lady* back on the touring boards than Cameron continued his new Arts Council partnership with a similarly lavish revival of *Oklahoma!*, also dedicated to the notion that regional theatres were entitled to the very best of Broadway instead of the usual pale imitations. This production also came triumphantly into the West End and then toured internationally. Now, nearly twenty years later, the Mackintosh Foundation is, in 1998, behind the new Trevor Nunn production at the National Theatre.

‘People often think musicals are just about good songs, but they're wrong’

'What happens when you work for months on shows as great as *My Fair Lady*, and *Oklahoma!* and *Oliver!* (not that there are that many others), is that you appreciate the incredible craft that lies in the construction of the book, the honing of the lyrics, the music, the arrangements, every single aspect of them. These shows are the summit of everything one strives for in the creation of a musical play: they remain as fresh as the day they were written, and when you consider in those shows the craft of Rodgers–Hammerstein or Lerner–Loewe or Lionel Bart, you realize there's not a wasted word in the book, not a lyric that doesn't inform the plot or characters and that all the music has a dramatic reason for being precisely where it is in the score. People often think musicals are just about good songs, but they're wrong. In the end, if the music isn't inherently dramatic, if there is no reason why it should be on stage rather than on radio or television, then you shouldn't go ahead. Even the dance music, the accents, the beats, the orchestrations are there to underpin the drama, like those great Agnes de Mille ballets in *Oklahoma!* Once I had worked for years and in detail on those three great scores, I was ready to begin on the new musicals I produced during the 1980s.'

In the summer of 1998 Rodgers and Hammerstein's revolutionary musical came back in triumph to the National Theatre in a production sponsored by the Mackintosh Foundation, directed by Trevor Nunn and choreographed by Susan Stroman. Inset – The 1979/80 Arts Council tour of *Oklahoma!* featured Alfred Molina (left) as Jud and John Diedrich as Curly. Above – Costume designs for the original performance.

But before that all started with a memorable punch-up, Cameron had one more pre-*Cats* show to do, and one that owed a considerable debt to *Side by Side by Sondheim*. Once again, this was to be an anthology of songs devoted to a single, living American composer–lyricist and, like Sondheim, one of the greatest. Tom Lehrer was then, and is still now, a Harvard professor of advanced mathematics who also found, in the late 1950s, that he had a considerable, if incongruous, talent for writing wonderfully witty cabaret songs all about the greater fallacies and lunacies of the 'American Way of Life'. These, for a while, he would perform himself to small concert audiences in and around Boston colleges, before cheerfully abandoning the stage piano and returning to his university lecture halls on the day Richard Nixon was elected President because, he said, he figured that satire could go no further than that.

His songbook and a few scarce concert recordings remained, however, and in 1980 it was Cameron, playing the Lehrer albums given to him by an American uncle as precious family heirlooms, who first realized that there might be a concert anthology in most of them. He approached Robin Ray, one of the early narrators of *Side by Side by Sondheim*, and together they came up with *Tom Foolery*, a joyous song-by-song-by-Lehrer celebration, which ran in the West End for nearly two years before being widely produced all over the world. Its deviser–producer still treasures the contract signed by Lehrer, which reads, in its entirety, 'I, Tom Lehrer, agree to sign this piece of paper in exchange for which Cameron Mackintosh agrees to send me several thousand pounds straight away, and additional large sums from time to time in the future.'

It was to be the beginning of a beautiful friendship, but until the gala performances of *Hey, Mr. Producer* in the summer of 1998 has never managed to get Lehrer himself back on stage.

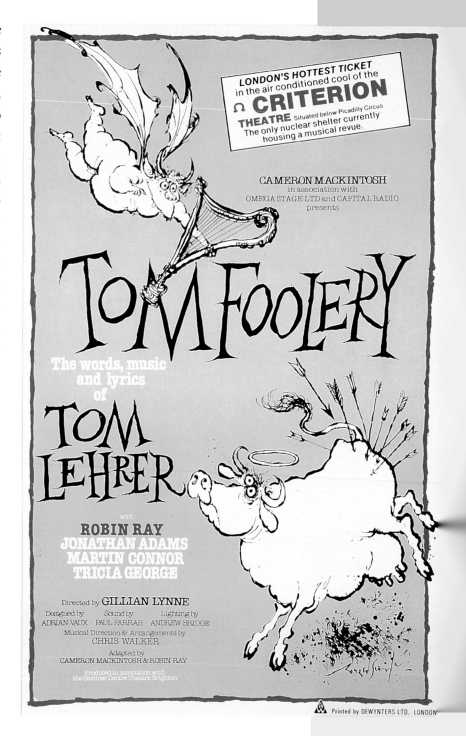

'Side by Side by Tom Lehrer'; 1980/81 – Cameron's next musical anthology was a brilliant compilation of the songs of the American satirist. Soon afterwards, when Richard Nixon was elected President, Lehrer retired from all personal appearances, announcing that satire could go no further. He was, however, to reappear for one night only at the 1998 charity gala which closes this book.

Trevor Nunn and Gillian Lynne in the original rehearsals for *Cats*; and (in front) the costume sketch for Gus the theatre cat, formally known as Asparagus.

6

GRIZABELLA GOES TO THE HEAVYSIDE LAYER

'And a new day has begun'

'Cats is, in fact, going to be a musical entirely about cats'

arly in 1980, Andrew Lloyd Webber rang Cameron Mackintosh and suggested a conciliatory lunch at the Savile Club. Cameron turned up, eager to meet the leading light of the British musical theatre, only to discover that they had an immediate rapport. Both men loved the musical theatre and vintage wine in roughly that order and discovered other points of contact. Besides, as Andrew had quickly realized, 'Anyone who can talk the Arts Council into financing a commercial tour of *My Fair Lady* knows quite enough about the fundraising of musicals for me.'

More or less of an age (Andrew is eighteen months younger than Cameron), they had both been introduced to musicals as small boys by theatrical relatives. Both were obsessives, both had built model theatres throughout their childhoods, and both now realized that they needed each other more than anyone else.

Over that one Savile lunch, a stage relationship was born which was to develop into the most important partnership for the musical theatre since that of Gilbert and Sullivan, another team not exactly immune to the occasional high-pitched backstage row.

As the new decade arrived, both men accepted their potential usefulness to each other at a time when both were at a crossroads in their musical careers. Andrew had enjoyed three triumphant West End and Broadway hits (*Joseph*, *Jesus Christ Superstar* and *Evita*) and thus far only one flop (*Jeeves*), but he had suddenly and recently lost his lyricist Tim Rice. Andrew had also decided, at the end of his contract with his producer, Robert Stigwood, to take his future into his own hands, in much the

same way that his idols, Rodgers and Hammerstein, had done after their successes with *Oklahoma!* and *Carousel;* and Stigwood, who had moved on to other non-theatrical showbiz interests in America, had also done. Cameron, at this equally crucial time in his career, was longing to do another original musical and had realized that he could hardly go on forever staging roadshow revivals of old classics or small-scale West End songbook anthologies.

Mackintosh had also astutely noticed before most others, that the Rice–Lloyd Webber partnership was over: 'The problem with them,' Cameron once observed, in perhaps the best instant summary of their always troubled alliance, 'is that Andrew can never wait to start on a new score, and Tim can never wait to get one finished so he can get back to the cricket.'

Now a potential new collaborator had turned up on the Lloyd Webber horizon, albeit in the unlikely shape of a dead poet. Some years earlier, at an airport bookstall before one of his many flights to America for *Superstar,* he had come across *Old Possum's Book of Practical Cats* by T. S. Eliot, the American poet who had himself spent several years as a dramatist. These poems, already familiar from childhood and now read to his own children, offered him something new. In the absence of a lyricist, here were ready-made verses for setting to music, but everybody he spoke to about this new idea thought he was mad.

As the American musical historian Michael Walsh points out, the idea was not in fact an entirely original one in that during Eliot's lifetime, the British composer Alan Rawsthorne had written incidental music over which the actor Robert Donat had read the poems. In

Valerie Eliot (left) with Cameron and the choreographer Gillian Lynne at the 1980 press conference which launched T. S. Eliot's *Old Possum's Book of Practical Cats* as a mega-musical. Mrs Eliot is clearly already aware of its potential, while Gillian and Cameron still look somewhat apprehensive.

Variations would be the first half and would use the poems like a modern *Façade* with a superstar like Liza Minnelli singing all the songs while dancers acted out the poems in the second half.'

What Andrew's faithful Sydmonton Festival audience saw, in that summer of 1980, was a tentative song cycle. It had no plot, no dramatic structure and no central characters. Lloyd Webber himself had not the faintest idea how to take it any further. Luckily, there was somebody in that audience who did. She was Valerie Eliot, once the poet's secretary, then his second wife and now his widow. She knew that Eliot would have loved Andrew's settings, and offered to hand over to him the entire correspondence surrounding the *Practical Cats*.

America, Walt Disney had already applied for the cartoon rights, to which Eliot retorted that his were hard-scrabble alleycats rather than old Uncle Walt's cute little kittens.

One unbeliever was the director Harold Prince, to whom Andrew first turned after their joint triumph with *Evita*. Hal took the view that *Cats* must be some kind of metaphor for a show about British political life. 'No, Hal,' said Andrew patiently over the transatlantic telephone to Broadway, '*Cats* is, in fact, going to be a musical entirely about cats.' For once, as he put down the receiver, Prince was speechless.

Back at that Savile Club lunch, Andrew had bemoaned the lack of good directors for musicals and Cameron remembered the work that Trevor Nunn had been doing at Stratford for the Royal Shakespeare Company – shows like *The Comedy Of Errors* and *Once in a Lifetime* had in fact been musicals in all but name. Andrew took Cameron home after lunch and played him some of the settings, and they agreed that their instincts were right, there was indeed something theatrical in there.

'I knew,' says Cameron, 'that I was the last producer Andrew had played any of the songs for, and at that time neither he nor I were sure whether he really had enough material for a full evening; so we explored a double bill where

'But the further down the line we got, the more letters and notes Valerie Eliot kept producing from her handbag. She even found some poems that had never been published but had been given to his nephews and nieces at Christmas, and her only real stipulation was that the whole thing should not end up like Beatrix Potter.' The combination of Valerie's trunk and Andrew's enthusiasm gave a still sceptical Trevor Nunn a tentative belief that there was a show to be done here after all, though his final commitment was still several months away.

At their first meeting, Trevor's reaction had been typical of the current showbiz thinking about *Cats* – Hal Prince had got *Evita*, Tom O'Horgan had got *Jesus Christ Superstar*, Frank Dunlop had got *Joseph* and here was he, head of the RSC, being offered the first Lloyd Webber that was certain to flop. But he didn't say no.

With Valerie's support and enthusiasm, Andrew went on worrying away at the project throughout the year, trying not only to complete the score for what had now become in his mind and hers a full-length musical, but also to interest backers in what seemed a daft project to everybody else. 'I see, you want to make a

West End musical out of poems by some dead guy who wrote *The Waste Land*, with cats instead of characters. Yeah, sure,' was a typical response. Not surprised, he had struck out with everyone he had so far tried.

'We knew from the very start,' says Cameron, 'that we had to make some kind of a cat's cradle on which to hang the poems, and at first we thought it might be some sort of a storyline like *Alice Through the Looking Glass*. Trevor was the first to realize that this would never work and, helped by Valerie's notes, he quickly found a tribal aspect to the show, having Grizabella as the loner who simply wants to rejoin her old community. That became our cat's cradle and by October I had brought on board not only Trevor but also my old associate Gillie Lynne, because I believed they were the only pair who could possibly pull it off. Trevor was equally keen to bring on board his RSC designers John Napier and David Hersey.'

Gillian Lynne had been Trevor's choreographer on his Stratford 'musicals' and was an inspired choice for *Cats*. A former ballet-turned-show dancer, Gillie had a strong visual sense and a dancer's knack for working out what the body could do without the movement becoming grotesque. Her signature was sinuous and smooth, with a way of fitting it into a theatrical framework which gave the plays she choreographed several additional dimensions. She also owned two dearly loved cats who were to become her models and inspiration.

Cameron's ongoing problems were financial, practical and geographic. And that was only the very beginning. There were many others. 'The second major problem was where we should do it. I had been looking at conventional theatres like Drury Lane and Her Majesty's when suddenly Andrew, doing a *This is Your Life* at the New London (then a television studio), rang me and said he had found the perfect space.' This was not then a widely shared view of the New

London. In the ten years since it was built on Drury Lane it had never had a single success, but the one thing going for it was Sean Kenny's radical theatre design. Cameron told the creative team that the risk was only justifiable if they believed they could design a set that could not be created in any other theatre.

Trevor Nunn and John Napier realized with excitement that in that space it was possible to build a unique set. In a miraculously short three months they came up with an extraordinary model entirely constructed of garbage and abandoned car parts. There were tyres and dustbins and assorted rubbish that reached throughout the auditorium. The entire space would became a colossal garbage dump scaled, not to human beings, but to the point of view of the show's feline characters.

By now the West End world was convinced that the whole *Cats* creative team had taken leave of its collective senses. These mad people with a Shakespearean director, who had never done a musical in his life, wanted to take some boring old poems into the unluckiest theatre in London. 'What we knew, very early in rehearsal,' says Cameron, 'was that we were doing something that should have happened in a back yard, but we were doing it in a big West End theatre using all our showbusiness forces. It was the most expensive workshop production in the world, and in the end it was going to be a shit or bust project. The brilliance of Trevor and John was to realize that they could make it an experience rather than just another musical. Their invention of the heavyside layer as a kind of heaven for old cats had only been a throwaway reference in Eliot, but for Trevor it became absolutely central to the show.

'At first, neither Andrew (who had agreed to go fifty–fifty on raising the capital) nor I could raise the money, and we only ever got it together in the last week of previews. Before rehearsals began Andrew had to give his per-

'Now and Forever' – The original cast of *Cats* on their way to the heavyside layer and the greatest smash hit in the history of the British musical at home and abroad.

be dancers. The original cast, assembled with some difficulty over the next few weeks, was to include Judi Dench (twenty years in the RSC but also the London star of *Cabaret*) as Grizabella. Once she had been persuaded to join by Trevor Nunn, to add some classical lustre to the company, it proved easier to convince other good actors that *Cats* had a chance. The heavy-set character actor Brian Blessed came in as Deuteronomy. With them were Gillian Lynne's old friend, the Royal Ballet principal Wayne Sleep, and London Festival Ballet's Ken Wells, together with the original Jesus and Judas of *Jesus Christ Superstar*, Paul Nicholas and Stephen Tate. Further down the cast list were also to be found the former child star Bonnie Langford and the former Pan's People dancer Sarah Brightman with whom, during the run, Andrew fell passionately in love and for whom he left his first wife, also named Sarah.

Of all the possible rehearsal nightmares, the one that happened was the one nobody expected. Judi Dench fell during one of the early rehearsals, injuring herself badly. On further examination it turned out to be a torn Achilles tendon which sent her straight to hospital. Previews, usually restricted to twelve, were extended for four weeks to give her time to recover and Judi was eager to come back until the run-through, about ten days before the first preview at Her Majesty's Theatre, where she slipped again. Confidence now shattered, it was clear that a replacement would have to be found urgently. There was one obvious choice. Elaine Paige, the star of Lloyd Webber's last musical hit *Evita*, was brought in over a weekend, just a few days before the first preview, and went on with only about four hours' stage rehearsal. This new presence created a whole new set of unforeseen backstage tensions.

Until this moment, Andrew's former and only living writing partner, Tim Rice, had stayed well away from a project which he, along with the

sonal guarantee of £75,000 to ensure that the theatre would honour its commitment, in return for which he asked an additional 5 per cent of the profits. I had thought that Andrew, with his fantastic track record, would have no trouble raising his half and that all the trouble would be with mine. But in fact we had equal difficulties. In the end we had to have 220 backers, which is an enormous amount, each putting an average of £750 into a show capitalized at £450,000.'

The last major problem was the casting. With just two exceptions (Old Deuteronomy and Grizabella herself) they would all have to

ʿWe were either going to be a complete hit or a complete fiasco̓

whole of theatrical London, still thought had been doomed from the outset. But now, with his lover called in to replace Dench, there was also the need to strengthen Grizabella's songs since Paige, unlike Dench, was primarily a singer rather than an actress.

The issue that arose was a new lyric for the opening of what was to become the show's greatest hit, 'Memory'. Andrew and Elaine asked Tim to come up with one in less than thirty-six hours. At the same time, however, Trevor Nunn, though not hitherto known as a lyricist, was working on his own version of some original Eliot poetry not being used in the show. Although both versions had been sung in preview Trevor, as director, had already decided to go with his own lyric, which he said was more Eliot-esqe. Not only was this deeply humiliating for Tim, so humiliating that it could be argued that his partnership with Andrew Lloyd Webber was mortally wounded there, then and forever, but that one simple choice was also radically to alter Nunn's bank balance for the rest of his life.

Tensions were inevitably high. What they were trying to create was something that they were constantly told did not and could not exist – a home-grown British dance musical. All Cameron's earlier experience had been on book shows like *Oliver!*, and of the entire creative team, only Gillian Lynne had any Broadway background.

Andrew had previously always had American directors – Hal Prince on *Evita* and Tom O'Horgan on the first production of *Superstar* – and was therefore understandably nervous of putting his first solo creation into the hands of Trevor Nunn, who had never directed a musi-

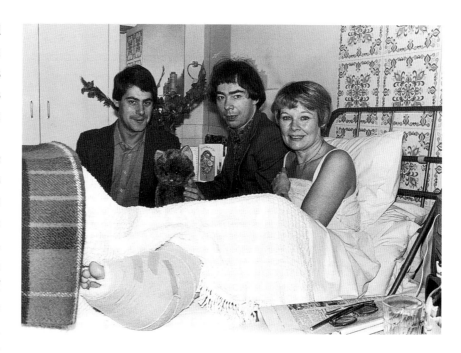

cal or, indeed, a major commercial production of any kind. But Cameron was sure he had made the right choice, and as rehearsals proceeded his director more than justified his faith: 'Trevor's main problem was that, because there was no plot, he really had nothing to direct until Gillian had got the whole show up on its feet; after that he could edit and fine-tune and push them through, because he is brilliant under fire. Trevor always does his best work in the last ten days before you open.'

Much was cut, moved, adjusted and re-thought during those last few rehearsals by every member of the team. Andrew in particular found the visualization of his brilliantly constructed score difficult. Cameron remained convinced about the genius of his new partner, 'Andrew automatically understands how a show should be put together; he's not as interested as I am in the detail but he is an extremely cunning musician, knows exactly where to place the right tune, and has a marvellous sense of structure.

Cats in crisis with less than a fortnight to go to the first preview, the star Judi Dench falls in rehearsal and fractures her ankle. Trevor and Andrew by her bedside (above) have to decide overnight whether to postpone or recast a production which the theatrical world was already writing off as a major feline flop. Reluctantly, they all realized that Judi was not going to make it in time, and only days before the opening, Elaine Paige (right) took over the role of Grizabella.

He makes sure there aren't any boring bits, compressing and compressing so that the show is composed from the first note of the overture to the end of the last encore. He's not much good with a set, but he can discuss all the other elements – unlike many composers he is a thoroughly theatrical animal. Whatever he may say about Hollywood, the theatre is all he lives and breathes for.

'What kept us going all through those fraught rehearsals was a kind of professional buoyancy,' says Cameron. 'Technical rehearsals seemed to go on forever but I knew we just had to go on with all guns blazing. To have had doubts would have been totally useless by that time. We were either going to be a major hit or a complete fiasco, and by the end of rehearsals I just wanted to get on and find out which. Even at the interval on the first night, when Andrew and I met in the bar, we still thought we had a total disaster.'

This then was the uncertain state of play on the night of 11 May 1981 when, after four weeks of sometimes shaky previews, *Cats* opened to the press. The first night itself was not exactly helped when, as Cameron remembers, 'Some drunk was shouting "Rubbish", which he thought was a funny comment on John Napier's set but luckily Lady Howe, sitting behind him, bashed him over the head with a very heavy handbag and told him if he even whispered in the second act she would do it again.' Things didn't improve when the theatre had to be evacuated at the curtain calls for one of the IRA bomb scares which were then current all over London. 'Never fear,' growled Milton Shulman of the *Evening Standard*. 'I'm not moving. This theatre has never had a hit yet.' It was the last night on which that could have been said.

NOW
AND
FOREVER

"Till the memory lives again"

❝Cats *meant that in theory I would never have to work again*❞

Reviews next morning, though not all ecstatic, were good enough to form queues at the box-office. The *Daily Telegraph* wrote of 'a ballet with songs, a musical with words to tickle the ear, and a stage spectacle to knock out the eye. Taking T. S. Eliot's *Book of Practical Cats*, the composer, Andrew Lloyd Webber has set them to jumpy, metallic tintinabulations, slithering snaky wails, and strongly percussive rhythms. Taking his music, the choreographer Gillian Lynne has got her company to dance with an electrifying sinuousity and vigour in costumes (by John Napier) that are the ultimate in feline chic. Taking all that, the director Trevor Nunn, has lavished a fortune on hidden lofts, roving spotlights and conjuring tricks which turn the round stage into a three-ring circus. In a word, the balance between Eliot's preoccupations with time and memory and Lynne's sheer outgoing exhilaration make for a purr-fect show.'

Though there were dissenters, notably Shulman for the *Evening Standard* who found it 'too arch and whimsical and feline', and James Fenton, the poet–critic of *The Sunday Times* who dismissed Eliot's work as 'drivel', there was a widespread feeling that something very special had happened at the New London and *Cats* quickly became the hottest ticket in town, overtaking even *Evita* and *Jesus Christ Superstar*.

Cameron is now philosophical about the opening. 'The whole nature of *Cats* was punctuated by a series of accidents and disasters, like the bomb scare and losing Dame Judi, but these things sometimes turn out right in the end. Because Elaine Paige is a singer who acts where Dame Judi is an actress who sings, the eventual rendering of 'Memory' was the catalyst for the

show, which might not have happened if it had been sung as originally intended by Judi.'

Cats was the show that gave Cameron Mackintosh creative respectability for the first time and which liberated Andrew from his dependence on any one collaborator. And the creative team – Gillian Lynne, Trevor Nunn, John Napier and one or two others – were redeemed in their faith in what all of London had thought was their stray cat-astrophe, by percentages which instead turned them all into millionaires.

Cats rocketed Cameron's career to a new level: 'I might always have gone on being a producer, but this was the show that overnight gave me financial security. Even though I had been producing for fourteen years I was still in debt when *Cats* opened, and the most important thing it did for me was to provide enough money that I now would only have to do the shows I really chose to do, and I could afford to nurture them for a very long time. It normally takes three or four years to put together a new musical; that costs a very great deal of money in development, and if you're having to work on other things in the meantime to make ends meet then you never give it enough attention. *Cats* meant that in theory I would never have to work again; but as I had never really cared about money, other than having enough to live and do another show, it didn't really alter the way I lived my life.'

Within ten days Andrew and Cameron realized that they had the biggest musical hit in town and they went immediately to America to sort out the Broadway opening, already confident

Left to right – Bonnie Langford,
Elaine Paige and Finola Hughes.

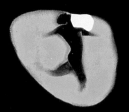

CATS

MUSIC BY ANDREW LLOYD WEBBER
BASED ON 'OLD POSSUM'S BOOK OF PRACTICAL CATS' BY T.S. ELIOT

NOW AND FOREVER

It is perfectly arguable that Cameron and Andrew may have both achieved better work in the seventeen years since *Cats* began, but the musical of T. S. Eliot's *Old Possum's Book of Cats* has underwritten and sustained everything that followed. It was quite simply the show that caused the rebirth of the British stage musical as effectively as *Oklahoma!* had, thirty years earlier, been the rebirth of Broadway.

that they had an iron-clad show. In the past, many musicals by Noël Coward, Lionel Bart, Leslie Bricusse and Sandy Wilson, to name but a few, had transferred successfully to Broadway, but in every case, the Shaftesbury Avenue creators and producers had simply sold foreign rights, allowing overseas buyers total control of the shows thereafter. The American budget came in at what was then a record-breaking $5 million, but instead of having to scratch around for every cent of it as they had in Britain, the Shubert Organisation simply handed them a single cheque for the whole amount for the rights and, most importantly, gave them *carte blanche* to reproduce their own staging.

As Lloyd Webber succinctly put it, 'A show doesn't open until it opens on Broadway,' and when *Cats* opened a year later at the expensively adapted Winter Garden Theater it had already taken an unprecedented $6 million at the advance box-office, a smash hit even before the reviews were written. It was already a genuinely critic-proof show.

At the age of thirty-four, Lloyd Webber had achieved something that not even Cole Porter or Rodgers and Hammerstein could ever have dreamed of. He had three musicals running simultaneously on Broadway where *Cats*, joined *Joseph* and *Evita*, and three more playing to capacity in the West End – again *Evita* and *Cats*, but by now also the brand new *Song and Dance*. During the run of *Cats* both he and Cameron were awarded knighthoods, not least for establishing the musical as the greatest commercial force in the history of British theatre at home and abroad.

The Japanese were also eager for the show, and by 1985 it had already travelled to Hungary, Austria, Canada and Australia as well. By the middle of that year it was running concurrently in its fourth London year, its third on Broadway and its second in Los Angeles, while a third American company was already on the road and rehearsals were underway in Norway and Finland. Cameron realized that he had hit the perfect international theme – there is, after all, nowhere in the world where people love theatre and hate cats.

So that's why cats. But why *Cats*? Why a show with no real plot, in which a large number of Jellical cats in lycra leg warmers pour on to a rubbish dump to tell a story that is at best fragmented and at worst non-existent?

There are several theories. One is that *Cats* created an entirely new audience of theatregoers, bored by increasingly tacky revivals of Rodgers and Hammerstein and eager for a mix of populism and innovation – in short, the event theory. Then again, it was the first British musical ever to be marketed as though it had come from Broadway or Hollywood. It could be argued that, despite his enormous care for the artistic product at every stage of production,

'A show doesn't open until it opens on Broadway'

from the initial idea to the distribution of merchandise, one of Cameron's major contributions to the theatre has been his insistence on image.

Each of his shows, starting with *Cats*, has had an immediately identifiable visual statement, a logo which has been used on everything even remotely connected with it wherever in the world it is. This is not to do with words or slogans. Those cat's eyes, which on closer examination are discovered to have dancers moving inside them, were mostly designed by Dewynters (as have been all of Cameron's show images) under the inspired creative imagination of Russ Eglin, and have a far greater public recognizability than the show's slogan, '*Cats*, Now and Forever', which was an American invention for the Shuberts. It is this instant identification which Cameron pioneered with *Cats* and continued with all his musicals. Within months of the opening night, his organization made sure you could buy badges, baseball caps, bookmarks, key-rings, musical boxes, T-shirts, mugs and watches, as well as the more traditional recordings, all bearing those cat's eyes. Indeed, merchandising now contributes considerably to *Cats* profits worldwide.

In all fairness, though, we should note here that at least some of the guidelines for *Cats* had been laid down before Andrew met up with Cameron Mackintosh. His previous producers on *Evita*, Robert Stigwood and the late David Land, had also begun to market their properties as never before.

What Cameron, whose main responsibility was the day-to-day production, did with *Cats* was to raise the international marketing of the British musical on to a quite different level. As soon as it became clear that *Cats* was, 'Now

and Forever', the production became a global event that even Cameron had never imagined it could be and Lloyd Webber became, for the first time, a global brand.

What this meant was that when you went into theatres in most major cities, you saw that same

Dewynters poster and, from Manchester to Melbourne, you saw exactly the same show. *Cats* was effectively and expensively reproduced around the world as exactingly as any can of Coca-Cola and wherever you saw it, the sensation was the same. He did this, not with a secret formula, but with one that was decidedly *not* secret. Nothing was left to chance. Offices were set up in America and Asia, with the London office remaining the European headquarters to maintain not just the brand leadership but also the quality of the product. For every critic who complained about the cloning, there were thousands of theatregoers around the world, fed up with getting fourth-rate touring companies of shows they had heard about but which singularly failed to live up to their advance publicity, now thrilled by the sight of one that was precisely the same in form, content and execution as the originals in London and New York. In those areas where Cameron knew it was neither suitable nor viable to reproduce the original, he would find appropriate local talents and organizations to make the shows work equally successfully in their territories. One of Cameron's innovations has been to develop teams of resident directors and choreographers whose job it is to maintain the quality of the creative team and keep the performers up to snuff – a task which used to be taken on by the stage management staff. These resident teams are charged with remounting the original productions in new locations, as well as maintaining the quality. As a result, *Cats*, *Phantom*, *Les Mis* and *Miss Saigon* in their second decade are invariably sharper and fresher than the average West End musical used to be once the replacement cast came in. Because of this painstaking attention, shows that might previously have run a few years are now lasting for decades.

Statistics now show that for the first eight years in London, when *Cats* ran without a single unsold seat, 35 per cent of the audience had come to it from overseas. Here for the first time was a musical without barriers of any kind. Dance is, after all, universal. There was no plot, but the characters were immediately recognizable to pet-lovers everywhere and the lyrics, as the work of one of our greatest poets, had already been translated into most European and Asian languages. For home audiences, before the show was ten years old, the hit song 'Memory' had been played on BBC television and radio 46,875 times. Audiences were coming to *Cats* singing the song on the way in. In publishing royalties alone the Nunn lyric was reckoned to have earned him, even by 1985, more than a million pounds, quite apart from the many millions from his directing fees for the versions which sprouted all around the world.

In 1981, incidentally, the lowest ticket price at the New London was £3 and the highest was £9.50. By 1997 those figures were £10.50 and £32.50. Backstage, in fifteen years *Cats* and its crew have used 31,875 headache pills; 35,625 posters; 450 radio microphones (it was *Cats* that pioneered the use of individual mikes for each on-stage singer, instead of group microphones at intervals on or above the stage); 449,283 throat pastilles; 3,900 pairs of shoes; 3,450 costumes for 270 dancers; 10,800 make-up sponges and 1,470 batches of lipstick, blusher and mascara.

Thanks to the constant worldwide restagings, *Cats* is still nowhere near its sell-by date. Casts are regularly replaced so that no dancer can be allowed to walk through the exceptionally difficult routines. Gus the Theatre Cat is still mourning his days with Henry Irving, countless new Grizabellas are still finding the same elegiac charm of 'Memory', Mr Mistopheles is still up to

"By much more than a cat's whisker, the show has now entered all theatrical history books"

his conjuring tricks and Macavity is still not there, in theatres from Seoul and Helsinki to Wichita and Wellington, which after fifteen years is not just a record but the smashing of records.

By much more than a cat's whisker, the show has now entered all theatrical history books, but we need to recall that the British invasion of Broadway, which began with *Cats* in the early 1980s, came at a unique time in the fortunes of Broadway itself. The triple threat of AIDS (which was to decimate an entire generation of dancers and singers, many of whom live in New York within a few blocks and beds of one another), increasingly recalcitrant unions and the decline of the Times Square environment into a dirty, druggy slum, had combined to create a vacuum into which Mackintosh moved with all possible speed. AIDS, while still prevalent, is being controlled by the gay community itself, while under Mayor Giuliani the Times Square area has been cleaned up, and the unions, having been badly frightened by the prospect of the Broadway theatre moving *en bloc* off Broadway, are now prepared to talk in millions instead of billions of dollars. So, had *Cats* been opening on Broadway in the autumn of 1997 it would have had considerably more local competition and might therefore perhaps not have been greeted with the generous and grateful acclaim that it actually received.

By the time *Cats* reached its fifteenth Broadway year, the native American industry had come back into its own with nearly a dozen new scores. But there were those who still resented the invasion that this show had launched. Many Broadway sages had grave doubts about the values of the British musicals. The actress and lyricist Gretchen Cryer was among the first to raise her head above the parapet, 'I must say I was enraged by *Cats* because I thought it was incredible sound and fury, signifying nothing, based on the merest filament of an idea. I immediately thought, "Let's go write a show about chandeliers called *Chandeliers* and have it about old chandeliers in old warehouses and everybody dressed up like a chandelier, singing songs about lighting up." *Cats* seems to me like taking the merest slip of an idea and putting millions of dollars into the icing when there's no cake there at all. I admit the physical production was done fantastically, but I was never touched or moved by it because I was so enraged by how top-heavy it had all become.'

If, in 1981, you had invested £10,000 in the first London *Cats,* by the summer of 1997 your return would have been just under £305,000. Other facts and figures around the time of the show's fifteenth birthday tell their own story. By January 1996 the show had taken a billion pounds around the world, of which £85 million came from London alone. The song 'Memory' has been recorded by more than one hundred different singers. Seven million people have seen *Cats* just in London. At any one time there are nine or ten productions playing simultaneously around the world. In 1989 it became the longest running musical in the West End and in 1997 it overtook *A Chorus Line* to achieve the same honour on Broadway. By that time, 8 million had paid $400 million to see it in New York while worldwide 50 million people had seen *Cats* in forty-two productions, grossing nearly £2 billion.

Cats was also by now proving a regular marriage market as well as a financial one. Lloyd Webber married Sarah Brightman and Trevor Nunn fell in love with another of the show's

'Broadway Babes' – On 19 June 1997, the original creators of *Cats*: (left to right) director Trevor Nunn, choreographer Gillian Lynne, designer John Napier, composer Andrew Lloyd Webber and producer Cameron Mackintosh, line up on stage to celebrate their show overtaking *A Chorus Line* as the longest running musical in the history of Broadway and the West End.

dancers, the British Demeter, Sharon Lee Hill, for whom he then left his long-time wife, Janet Suzman while, not to be outdone, John Napier fell in love with the American Demeter.

The phenomenon of *Cats* was ultimately down to its classical heritage. Trevor Nunn, coming off the triumphant RSC *Nicholas Nickleby*, had already some idea of what was required from a stage picture and Mackintosh, already talented in putting together apparently disparate groups of people, had also brought in Richard Stilgoe to boost some of the early lyrics. Still only in their early thirties, Cameron and Andrew were now the hottest kids on the English block, but their problem was precisely where to go from here.

The interest in the show was worldwide but here, for the first time, was a musical originating in London, of Broadway proportions yet without the involvement of any single American, except David Hersey, a long-time resident of the UK. Hitherto, the British musical had been essentially a cottage industry. With one feline leap it had become a worldwide web. Gillian Lynne, who had choreographed the show on British-trained dancers, was over-

whelmed by the level and depth of dance talent on Broadway. With a tradition of dance-based shows behind them, the American dancers had a flexibility and adaptability she had never before experienced and she remade the dances to accommodate the raised expectations. She then took them back to London and made her British dancers rise to the challenge.

When they took *Cats* to Broadway they still had to make many allowances for American audience susceptibilities; the show became louder and larger but lost much of its original melancholy menace and, as in London, the reviews were somewhat mixed. Frank Rich for the *New York Times*, talked of 'theatrical magic', but Brendan Gill for the *New Yorker*, found it 'a mighty spectacle about mighty little'.

Lloyd Webber, always quicker than Cameron to take up the cudgels against the American press, noted, 'Americans just don't like a British team coming over with a musical when that is what they are supposed to do best over here. We were expecting that reaction but, believe me, we shall be here for years to come.'

At the time of this writing, seventeen years later, the show is still strong on Broadway, as elsewhere, and even though some elaborate plans to film it, either with a Tom Stoppard screenplay or a Spielberg animation, have so far come to nothing, the video of the original stage show has now been released.

But then, in 1982, with *Cats* firmly established on both sides of the Atlantic and setting off on its royal progress around the world, it was time for Cameron to turn his attention to other projects. At Sydmonton that year, Andrew had spoken with Cameron about rolling on with Trevor Nunn to *Starlight Express*, but Mackintosh, with *Cats* taking off worldwide, didn't have time to do another epic quite yet and was more intrigued by the potential fun of two small shows – Tim Rice's *Blondel* and Ashman and Menken's *Little Shop of Horrors*.

VARIATIONS ON SEVERAL THEMES

"Suddenly Seymour"

'It smelt just perfect, and luckily once again my intuition worked'

The Tom Lehrer celebration, *Tom Foolery*, was offered a New York production and gave Cameron the opportunity to dip his producer's toe into the uncharted New York waters a year before *Cats* opened there. *Tom Foolery* repeated its London success and through it he met Albert Poland, the show's general manager. Via him Cameron got involved with a still more eccentric project, *Little Shop of Horrors*, which he took sight unseen when Poland phoned him with the plot synopsis of the workshop, based, of course, on Roger Corman's kitsch and cliquey low-budget horror movie about a dentist and a people-eating plant from Outer Space that threatens to

Suddenly Seymour; 1982/3 – Sarah Payne, David Burt and Barry James (above) and Ellen Greene (left) in the Ashman–Menken *Little Shop of Horrors*. Cameron produced the show on both sides of the Atlantic after it had been a hit cult movie. Sadly, Ashman died of AIDS a few years later, but Alan Menken has gone on to become the resident composer for Disney's animated classics.

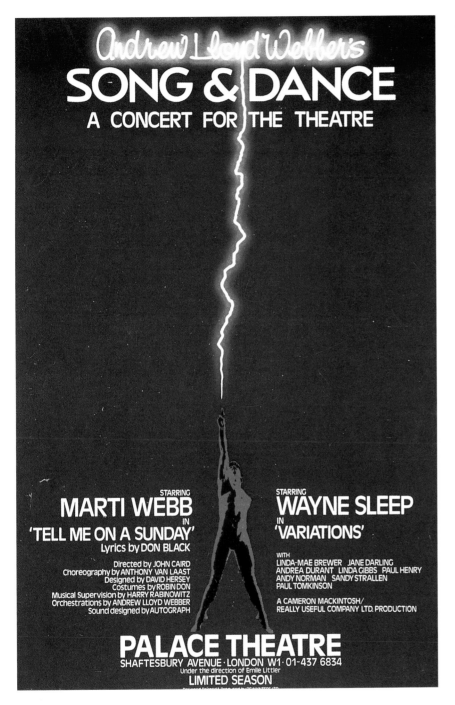

take over the world. 'It smelt just perfect, and luckily once again my intuition worked. *Little Shop of Horrors* ran more than four years off Broadway, another two in London and only ever flopped in California, where they had never seen anything funny about dentistry.'

So once again Cameron's luck was in. *Little Shop of Horrors* was the most internationally successful off-Broadway musical since *The Fantasticks* and it launched its writers, Howard

Ashman (lyrics) and Alan Menken (music), on a triumphant career which ultimately led them to Hollywood and Disney, an association cut short only by Ashman's tragic AIDS death at the age of forty in the same year they won an Oscar for *The Little Mermaid.* Ironically, his successor as Menken's lyricist at Disney was to be Andrew's former partner, Tim Rice.

Andrew was never entirely happy when there was only one new score on the piano and during the long run-up to *Cats* he had started working on an entirely different project, a song cycle about a young English girl trying to make it in a hostile New York world. With Tim Rice already backing away as fast and far as he could from the Lloyd Webber orbit, Andrew now began to work with Don Black, the English lyricist who had already made his name around London's Tin Pan Alley substitute, Denman Street, with songs for Matt Munro and three of the James Bond title songs with John Barry. Black had once lived in California and eagerly came up with lyrics like 'Capped Teeth and Caesar Salad' for an hour-long show which was again the hit of Lloyd Webber's Sydmonton Festival and was subsequently televised in February 1980 with Marti Webb as the young woman on the make in the big city.

Andrew had written his version of *Variations on a Theme* by Paganini for his cellist brother, Julian, and it had become famous as the theme for Melvin Bragg's *South Bank Show.* But neither this nor *Tell Me on a Sunday* had ever seemed to Andrew to have any kind of theatrical life, even though he had put on a successful *Tell Me on a Sunday* concert at the Royalty Theatre. Not, that is, until he and Cameron, on the boat to New York after the triumphant London opening of *Cats* (to decide which of the many suitors was to be allowed to produce *Cats* there), began to look to the future. As Andrew asked him whether there was anything he could now do with *Tell Me on A Sunday,*

Mackintosh replied, 'Yes, put it together with *Variations*. We could then call the whole show *Song and Dance*.'

And that was precisely what they now proceeded to do at the Palace Theatre, at least in part for sentimental reasons – Cameron had been a stage manager there while Andrew, already into architecture, was in love with the building. They put it in for what was intended as a twelve-week filler season, mainly to keep the Palace Theatre open. Andrew and Don reworked *Tell Me on a Sunday* so that the songs told the story of a girl and her unhappy American romance, and Wayne Sleep, the principal dancer in *Cats*, danced the second half of the show *Variations*, against a background of the skyscrapers and fire escapes of New York.

The show did not exactly take critics by storm ('It is a very long time since I have had to sit through a more ostentatious, less theatrically coherent evening' – Michael Coveney, the *Financial Times*), but by dropping into the first half a series of different guest stars from the original Marti Webb – through Lulu and Liz Robertson to Sarah Brightman – Mackintosh kept the show alive at the Palace for almost 800 performances before they took it back to television with Brightman now in the lead, although neither Cameron nor Andrew thought this version right for Broadway.

In 1983 Cameron got involved with Tim Rice and the composer Stephen Oliver in what was intended to be a small-scale historical satire on the lines of Rice's original *Joseph and the Amazing Technicolour Dreamcoat*. In the intervening ten years, however, everybody had got more ambitious and *Blondel* now

1982 – Double bill: Lloyd Webber and Cameron decide on a concert for the theatre which would pair *Tell Me on a Sunday*, the Don Black–Lloyd Webber score about a girl at large in a hostile New York, with *Variations*, the Wayne Sleep dance piece based on *Variations on a Theme* by Paganini. Cameron and Wayne Sleep (above) renewing a partnership that went back to *Cats* and (left) Andrew on the piano with Marti Webb, the original star, and John Caird, the director.

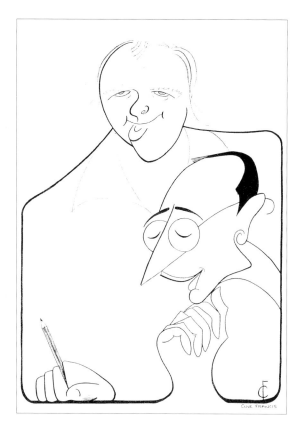

both *Cats* and *Song and Dance* running in the West End, it was hardly surprising that Tim Rice should also feel the need to follow *Evita* with another blockbuster. The problem was that although *Blondel* was to have a great many of Cameron's and Tim's newly minted five-pound notes spent on its production, the score had been conceived as a successor not to *Evita* or *Superstar* but to *Joseph*, and the simplicity of the writing contrasted badly with a too-lavish Tim Goodchild medieval setting, a set which in fairness was designed to accommodate anything that Rice would come up with. The best that the *Daily Telegraph* could find to say in the show's favour was, '*Blondel* is a good-natured romp which nevertheless failed to hit the heights' and other reviews were a good deal worse than that one.

And it was now that Cameron, albeit tem-

1983 – 'Saladin Days': the late Stephen Oliver and Tim Rice (drawn here by Clive Francis) as rehearsals began for *Blondel*, one of Cameron's least successful 1980s musicals. The wandering minstrel show starred Paul Nicholas in a medieval mystery tour, which came to a grinding halt soon after transferring to the West End from the Old Vic.

emerged to reopen the Old Vic as an epic musical about the wandering minstrel of the title. Stephen Oliver's background had been entirely operatic and although Tim Rice managed one or two very witty lyrics (not least 'Saladin Days'), it was clear from the outset that the show was a loser.

Looking back on this 'white and white' minstrel show, years later, Cameron noted, '*Blondel* managed to run fifteen months at the Vic and then the Aldwych and it lost its entire investment, largely because we went into rehearsal only a few days after a script was delivered (Tim is always a deadline writer) and therefore we had no chance of the pre-production year or two that big musicals must have between writing and staging. We simply didn't have the time to get it right, and the production ended up far too big and heavy for its score. It should have been a much smaller show, and then Tim's brilliant charm and wit would not have been so horribly lost.'

It was true. Now that Lloyd Webber had

porarily, ran out of luck with one of his favourite shows. He was asked to transfer *Oliver!* from London to New York, where Ron Moody made his Broadway debut as Fagin, with Patti Lupone as Nancy, but the crucial *New York Times* review was negative and it failed to find an audience, closing after a mere eight weeks.

'Blondel is a good-natured romp, which nevertheless failed to hit the heights'

That certain thing called *The Boy Friend*.

His next two shows did not fare very much better. Cameron had been invited to reopen the Old Vic after one of its periodic closures for refurbishment and, he decided to do so with a new production of Sandy Wilson's *The Boy Friend*, which, alongside *Salad Days*, had been the great British musical hit of the 1950s. But although the show had started its life in 1953 at the miniscule Players Theatre and had gone seriously wrong only on the two occasions when it was blown up out of all proportion against the author's wishes (first for Broadway and then for a characteristically eccentric Ken Russell movie), Mackintosh still felt that if they were to fill the stage as well as the stalls of the Vic they would again have to try doing it big.

Neither Wilson nor the critics were very happy with the outcome. Admittedly, things had not been made easier by the departure of Glynis Johns before the show ever came into London. Surprisingly Wilson did not remove his name from the credit of 'Production Supervisor', even though this revival yet again tried to blow up a very small concept to somewhere dangerously near puncture. The director of this revival, Christopher Hewett (a compromise candidate of Sandy's after he had turned down Trevor Nunn, Mike Ockrent and Alan Strachan), seemed to have at least one eye on the current Broadway success of *My One and Only* in particular, and on tap-dance nostalgia in general. Somewhere along the line, it had lost the charm of its original production and failed to find a new voice.

The Boy Friend came only a few months after *Abbacadabra*, a charming but extremely expensive children's show made up of hits by the soft-rock group ABBA, with a cast headed by Elaine Paige and B. A. Robertson. 'We did a hugely successful Christmas at the Lyric, Hammersmith, but the show was desperately expensive to run and I couldn't find a way of making it work out of the holiday season,' said Cameron, looking back.

But what was truly amazing about *Abbacadabra* were the six writers involved. Two of them were, of course, Bjorn Ulvaeus and Benny Andersson of the original ABBA, who were to go on to write *Chess* with Tim Rice. The other four were the English lyricist Don Black, soon to be much involved in Andrew's later musicals, the children's playwright David Wood, with whom Cameron had been working for some years, and the creators of the original concept album. These were two unrelated Frenchmen with the same last name: Daniel Boublil, who then disappeared without trace, and Alain Boublil, who was to prove hugely influential in Cameron's subsequent career.

1983 – Despite an impressive cast (Elaine Paige, B. A. Robertson, Phil Daniels, Michael Praed) and a distinguished production team (author David Wood, lyrics Don Black, music and original book by ABBA), *Abbacadabra* was a musical adventure that survived only a brief Christmas season at the Lyric, Hammersmith. One name on the programme was, however, to influence the rest of Cameron's career: the co-author of the book, Alain Boublil.

Les Misérables at the barricades: a revolution in France and in world theatre.

9

VICTOR VICTORIOUS

"Do you hear the people sing?"

❝It was an instant, combustible decision. By the fourth track I had already decided that I had to do it❞

Alain Boublil, born 5 March 1941 in Tunis, had come to Paris to be a songwriter and music publisher but his passion was the musical theatre. An experienced lyricist, he had a hand in a number of French pop songs of the 1960s and 1970s, but was already becoming bored with the three-minute form. With his friend, the composer Claude-Michel Schönberg (born in Vannes in Brittany, 5 July 1944, a distant relative of the twelve-tone inventor Arnold Schönberg), who was also anxious to move into a more serious musical sphere, Boublil had put together, in 1973, an amazing pageant called *La Revolution Française*. Its first airing was at the Palais des Sports in Paris, with Schönberg himself appearing as Louis XVI. It ran for its scheduled sixteen-week season, after which Alain and Claude-Michel returned to the pop music business.

Both Boublil and Schönberg were still working as producers in the French record industry in a country that has never really accepted any contemporary musical theatre. But whenever they were in London or New York on business they would make a point of going to see such shows as *Jesus Christ Superstar*, wondering all the time why a similar musical project could never be made to succeed in their adopted hometown of Paris.

In 1978 Boubil came to London to see a show that he had fallen in love with as a movie. It was, as it turned out, Cameron's production of *Oliver!* and, as the Artful Dodger sang 'Consider Yourself', the character of Gavroche, the Paris urchin in Victor Hugo's classic French novel, *Les Misérables*, came unbidden into his mind. By the end of that per-

formance, Boublil claims, the outline of what was to become one of the musical theatre's greatest hits had begun to emerge. After the final curtain he ran to the telephone to tell his partner, Claude-Michel, that he had a subject for their next show.

Energized by this, they then, against all advice, took the next ten months off from their paying jobs to formulate, write, record and deliver a concept album of *Les Misérables* and it was this that the great French director, Robert Hossein, heard. He was sufficiently impressed to make it into a dramatic musical tableau, again for the Palais des Sports. Somewhere during this run they made a tape.

A couple of years later this recording was picked up by a young Hungarian director, Peter Farago, who took it to the one British producer who, he now reckoned, had the background

Alain Boublil, Cameron and Claude-Michel Schönberg keeping their eyes on the future of *Les Misérables*.

and the resources to stage it. Mackintosh had, however, serious doubts about Farago as director and made it clear from the outset that although he would of course get a scouting fee, Cameron was not prepared to take on *Les Mis* (as it was already becoming known across the Channel) if the deal had to include Farago. They agreed and as soon as he had a moment, Cameron listened to the recording. 'It was,' says Cameron now, 'an instant combustible decision. By the fourth track I had already decided that I had to do it.'

That same day, Mackintosh took it to Alan Jay Lerner, whose producer he had recently been on the last *My Fair Lady*. The two of them listened to the record but Lerner, already ailing, declined to adapt *Les Mis* and write the English lyrics. 'I think it's terrific but it's just not for me,' he said, 'I write about people's dreams, and this is about people's suffering.'

After Lerner, Mackintosh took it to Howard Ashman (of *Little Shop Of Horrors* fame), who loved it but said it, too, wasn't for him, and then to Sheldon Harnick, who memorably dismissed it as a 'non-starter'. Still undeterred and enthusiastic, Cameron went to Paris to meet Alain and Claude-Michel at the beginning of 1983 and there began perhaps the most important friendship and professional collaboration of his life. Traditionally, French composers, songwriters and indeed playwrights simply sell rights across the Channel or the Atlantic. On this occasion, however, it soon became clear that Cameron had a much more extensive and intimate plan of collaboration. He wanted to take the two Frenchmen on a journey through the British and American theatre as equal collaborators. This would, of

course, have to start with an appropriate anglophone lyricist.

Then chance intervened. The poet and drama critic of London's *The Sunday Times*, James Fenton, had just had a big success adapting *Rigoletto* as a Mafia thriller for Jonathan Miller at the Coliseum, and Cameron was one of thousands of non-opera-goers who suddenly found in Fenton the key to what had always been a locked door. He now approached James with the idea that he should be the one to take on *Les Mis*. Fenton agreed to the task but, characteristically, then spent the summer on a canoe in Borneo with a university friend who was writing a book. He took Victor Hugo's novel with him and, as he proceeded through the hefty tome, he tore off the chapter he had just read and fed it to whatever wildlife was swimming past the canoe at the time. Not surprisingly, with these distractions, it took him a very long time to finish the book.

From the beginning, Cameron had decided that the only possible choice to bring *Les Mis* to life would be his *Cats* director, Trevor Nunn, who now had the experience of a major musical to add to his and John Caird's classic eight-hour *Nicholas Nickleby*. Only they, Cameron believed, could combine the seriousness of the classical theatre, which the great French novel deserved, with the theatricality of the wide-stage musical epic.

'I went round for breakfast to Cameron's flat,' Nunn later told the journalist Edward Behr, 'and he played me the record. Before he did so we talked about the novel, which I had to confess I had never read. Cameron then proceeded to tell me the story of *Les Misérables*. He said it was all about a convict, hunted and chased for the whole of his life by an obsessed policeman – a nineteenth-century version of *The Fugitive*, in fact. Subsequently I discovered that Cameron had not read *Les Misérables* either and that his was a somewhat inaccurate digest. There is more to *Les Mis* than that. But his conversation left me the impression of a simple, driving, theatrical, dramatic motor force which stayed with me far longer than the original recording.'

Nunn, for his part, made two demands. The first was to have far-reaching consequences in the financial life of the RSC and, of course, Trevor himself. He insisted that the show must open the RSC Barbican season in the autumn of 1984, with Cameron as co-producer. After a run at the Barbican Cameron could then transfer it to the West End but, even then, should it survive commercially, a percentage of all profits in perpetuity would go back to the RSC. This, in short, was Trevor's way of squaring his conscience with the RSC leadership at a time when both he and Peter Hall at the National were coming under press fire for their extra-curricular activities. Happily, that agreement, though frowned upon by the rest of the RSC administration, was, over the next fifteen years, to prove on more than one occasion the difference between the RSC in credit and the RSC in debt. His second demand, easily satisfied, was that, as with *Nickleby*, he should have John Caird as co-director.

For his part, Cameron insisted that although the partnership wih the RSC would indeed provide a considerable artistic input (an unusually lengthy ten-week rehearsal period), the show should be treated in all other respects as a commercial West End venture. *Les Misérables* was, in other words, not to be slotted into an autumn repertoire but to stand totally apart as an eight-week nightly run on the main stage. It was also to be designed to fit into its eventual West End home, the Palace Theatre, rather

Co-directors Trevor Nunn and John Caird in rehearsal for *Les Misérables*.

than for the larger and more unwieldy space of the Barbican Theatre. The responsibility for casting and musical decisions was Cameron Mackintosh's (in consultation with the RSC), rather than the more widely bruited notion that the Mackintosh Office was simply accepting an RSC production for transfer.

Fenton returned from his travels with a rough draft of the English lyrics, or at least the first act. But because of the unusual circumstances of the writing, he was only halfway through the libretto. A 1984 opening at the Barbican was clearly off the agenda. Mackintosh elected to delay for a year. Fenton continued to work on the lyrics all though 1984 and during this period John Caird, a close friend of Fenton's, worked with him to encapsulate the lyrics into dramatic form. Equally, James was meeting regularly with Alain Boublil.

It wasn't until December, in a wintry Stratford-upon-Avon, that auditions for the show finally began and the production team had to then face the most difficult decision they had so far encountered. It had become finally and painfully clear to all that the poet in James Fenton was too isolated and solitary a figure to fit into the elaborately collaborative machinery of a modern mega-musical such as *Les Mis-*

Costume designs for *Les Mis* by Andreane Neofitou.

érables. It needed a much more mainstream and experienced musical writer.

Cameron found one in Herbert Kretzmer, former drama critic on the *Daily Express* and now *Daily Mail* television critic, whom he knew only slightly as the author of *Our Man Crichton*. Cameron remembered that he was also the lyricist who had translated Charles Aznavour's French songs into English. Above all, he was the writer of at least three small-scale West End musicals.

It was already January 1985, and Kretzmer's brief was to deliver a complete English adaptation by the middle of June so that rehearsals could start for what was to be an October 1985 opening at the Barbican.

With considerable courage, on the day that Mackintosh made him the offer, Kretzmer resigned from the *Daily Mail*, holed himself up in his Basil Street flat with Nunn and Caird's scenario and worked around the clock with Claude-Michel and stacks of smoked salmon from the Harrod's Food Hall across the road. 'I had never worked so hard at anything in my life,' says Kretzmer. 'There was an enormous amount of writing still to be done. What I was now engaged to do cannot in any way be called just translation. A third of the work to be done consisted of a form of indirect translation, a third was free adaptation with completely new words to existing music and a third of it involved writing completely new songs.'

Indeed, the original Paris staging of *Les Misérables* had run little more than an hour, whereas the new version, if they were lucky, would come in at about three and a half hours. Kretzmer's hard work ultimately paid handsomely, and even Fenton was given a percentage for his input, which over the years has amounted to millions of pounds. However, Herbert Kretzmer has always felt shortchanged in the advertising, and to this day often has to fight for his third share of the

billing. From Cameron's point of view, Boublil and Schönberg are the sole creators of *Les Misérables*, and remain its sole progenitors. For the first time, Cameron was dealing with musical writers who were effectively his own discoveries, and from now on, although he would continue to work (albeit less closely) with Lloyd Webber and many other composers, it was undoubtedly Boublil and Schönberg whom he took to his heart and on whose musicals he effectively rests his case as producer.

In the musical theatre history of this century, given average theatregoing luck, once in every five or ten years a musical soars out across the pit, providing a feast for the eyes as well as the ears. *Les Misérables* is one such, a great blazing pageant of life and death at the barricades of political and social revolution in the nineteenth-century France of Victor Hugo.

But quite apart from Victor Victorious, what matters about *Les Misérables*, like Britten's *Peter Grimes* and Sondheim's *Sweeney Todd*

'Who will be strong and stand with me?' To the barricades of *Les Misérables*.

(and for that matter Verdi's *Rigoletto* but precious little else), is that it sets out to redefine the limits of musical theatre. Like them, it is through-sung, and like them it tackles universal themes of social and domestic survival in terms of individual despair. When the show first opened in its Parisian sports arena in 1980, its score already seemed to consist of all the great marching songs that Edith Piaf somehow never got around to singing. There is an energy and an operatic intensity that exists in the work of no British composer, past or present: the sense of a nation's history being channelled through trumpets and drums and violins and guitars and cellos. These songs, ranging from the joyously hilarious 'Master of the House' to the haunting 'Empty Chairs at Empty Tables', tell of love and war, death and restoration, together with duets and chorus numbers of dazzling inventiveness.

For this is not the French equivalent of *Oliver!* nor yet the musical of *Nicholas Nickleby*, though it owes a certain debt to both. Rather *Les Mis* is a brilliantly guided tour of the 1,200-page eternity of Victor Hugo's text, and indeed there is no way that in three orchestral hours one could ask for more than that. The chase through Parisian sewers (in the manner of *The Third Man*) is here, as is an autumnal ending worthy of *Cyrano de Bergerac*. There are even a few lovable orphans faintly reminiscent of *Annie*, and the result is a fragmentary, episodic evocation of other shows and other countries. For no musical exists in a vacuum. Just as John Napier's rich and rare set is made up of old treasures – chairs, tables, cart wheels

Members of the original Barbican cast: Alun Armstrong, Colm Wilkinson, Susan Jane Tanner with one of the first Cosettes.

water barrels – so the whole production reflects what Nunn and his co-director had learnt from *Nickleby* and *Cats* and their Shakespeare-based musicals.

But *Les Misérables* does more than just draw on its own theatrical and political origins. Like the best of Bernstein and Sondheim, it also pushed the boundaries of music theatre forward, so that it exists in the most dangerous area of the footlights. Like *West Side Story*, this is not a show about glamour or success. And yet, as its score surges through the theatre, one is made aware again and again of how triumphantly it works, somewhere at the boundaries of not only Hugo, but also Dickens and Brecht.

Les Misérables is everything the musical theatre ought to be doing; it relies on no gimmicks

Michael Ball and Frances Ruffelle in rehearsals for *Les Misérables*.

of choreography, no repetitive phrasing, no simplistic homilies, no eleven o'clock number. It is not even a star show, though the first London stagings at the Barbican and the Palace did contain superlative central performances from Patti LuPone and Colm Wilkinson and Roger Allam and Alun Armstrong, actors drawn equally from the worlds of rock opera and classical theatre, and it also launched the careers of such as Michael Ball and Frances Ruffelle. The history of the British subsidized theatres' attempts to do musicals has not been a happy one, from the shambles of *Jean Seberg* to the catastrophe of *Carrie*. But with *Les Mis*, for the very first time, the artistic resources of the RSC came together with the artistic, financial and entrepreneurial talents of Cameron Mackintosh and, if the first half of this century gave us *Porgy and Bess*, then its only natural successor in the second half has been *Les Misérables*.

None of this, however, was apparent on that first opening night at the Barbican in 1985. Late rehearsals had become very fraught, not least because Trevor was refusing to make the cuts which Cameron felt essential for a West End run. As for the critics, they for the most part didn't care for any of it. In rejecting the old established star system (both Topol and Max von Sydow had been turned down) Cameron was running the risk of an unsellable show, and the morning after the first night the production team – Cameron and Trevor plus John Napier on sets and David Hersey on lights – gloomily read reviews that were, in Nunn's simple definition, 'killers'.

Cameron, with the hostile reviews now all in, had to decide irrevocably whether to go for the West End. The advance at the Barbican was still minimal and on all sides he was being advised to let the show die a quiet RSC death. He now faced the most crucial decision of his entire working life. Within forty-eight

"Les Misérables *is everything the musical theatre ought to be doing*"

Early and tentative artwork for the *Les Misérables* poster and logo; the influence of the theatrical design agency Dewynters and especially of their longtime leading artist Russ Eglin has always been central to the very beginning of the creative process on a Mackintosh show.

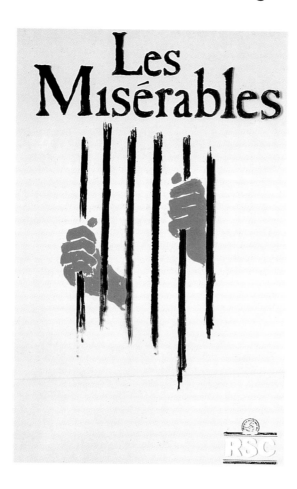

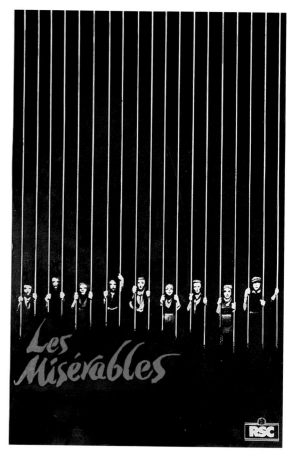

hours of those reviews hitting the streets, he had to decide whether to invest a further £300,000 in transferring the show from the Barbican to his own management at the Palace, or whether to cut his losses and close at the Barbican, thereby losing only his £50,000 deposit, plus, of course, an entire two years of his working life.

Everybody, it seemed, was against moving *Les Mis* into the West End. Everybody, that is, except Cameron, Boublil and Schönberg, and Herbert Kretzmer, who could not believe that all their work was to end up in a three-month run at the Barbican. And, crucially, Cameron's two principal backers said they would continue to back him all the way if he decided to bring it in. He called the manager of the Barbican box-office, who reported a curious phenomenon. 'Mr Mackintosh,' he said, 'I think you ought to know that since ten o'clock this morning there has been a queue snaking all around the Barbican. All of them want tickets for *Les Mis*.' That was all Cameron needed to hear.

But he had yet another problem. Although the Palace had long been their chosen West End destination, it had recently been bought by Andrew Lloyd Webber, who not only hated *Les Misérables* but was also eager to keep his own new stage clear for an equally epic project on which he was still working, his musical of *The Phantom of the Opera*. But Andrew, whose associates at the Palace, Brian Brolly and Biddy Hayward, had always been much more supportive of *Les Mis* than he himself, had to

The etching of the orphan child from an early edition of Victor Hugo's *Les Misérables* became, a century later, the symbol of Cameron's risky but ultimately triumphant transfer of the show from the Barbican to the Palace (right), and then later to the vast open spaces of the Toronto SkyDome (below).

accept that *Phantom* was still a year from production and that *Les Mis* could, indeed would, transfer to the Palace as contracted early in December.

And not everybody hated the show – even those who had nothing to do with its production or eventual transfer. There were one or two of us among the West End critics who fell immediately and deeply in love with it, and went on writing about it week after week in the face of much opposition. As Trevor Nunn was good enough to note later, 'these very few raves, repeated as they were in international papers, were our lifeline. Very soon we started getting enquiries from Japan and the USA about the possibility of taking the show abroad.'

In the thirteen years that have elapsed since

Gouda Luck !

OPENS TONIGHT IN AMSTERDAM

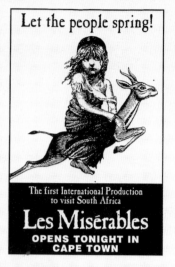

Let the people spring!

The first International Production
to visit South Africa

Les Misérables

OPENS TONIGHT IN
CAPE TOWN

A REVOLUTIONARY EVENT PREMIERES
TONIGHT IN BOSTON

LOS ANGELES GETS ITS OWN REVOLUTION ON JUNE 1

We're saving a seat for you at the Imperial Theatre.

Los Misérables.

Premieres tonight in Madrid

Sweeping down
the Rhine

Prost!

OPENS TONIGHT IN
DUISBURG GERMANY

Premieres tonight in Honolulu

Fantastic!

PREMIERES IN SINGAPORE
TONIGHT

100

101

Welcome Home !

its opening, *Les Mis* has taken more than £20 million in London alone. It has now been seen worldwide in more than fifty productions, from Toronto to Tokyo by way of Rekjavik and soon Rio, as well as triumphantly in concert versions. In the programme for one of these productions, an all-star tenth anniversary gala at the Royal Albert Hall which united casts from all over the world, Cameron for the first time wrote his own thoughts about the show.

'Until I heard the original French album of *Les Misérables* in 1982 I had always considered the idea of a French musical a contradiction in terms. The French have hardly ever taken to modern musicals, and Paris has proved the early graveyard for most of the worldwide musical successes of the last fifty years; they prefer revivals of operettas, Euro-rock musicals of dubious origin and the occasional short, chic season of American touring musicals – performed in English. How two Frenchmen, Claude-Michel Schönberg and Alain Boublil, managed not only to survive in such an alien culture but also write one of the greatest musicals of all time is a miracle.

'Perhaps the best explanation for the enormous success of *Les Misérables* comes from Victor Hugo himself, when he wrote to his publisher: "You are right, Sir, when you say *Les Misérables* is written for a universal audience. I do not know whether it will be read by everyone, but it is meant for everyone."'

Suitably enough, it is Claude-Michel Schönberg who gets the last word on the universal aspects and ongoing international triumph of *Les Mis*: 'Our characters are composed of all the archetypes of human society – every community, every major organization, almost any

group, has its Javerts, its Thenardiers and its Fantines, and every one of us longs to be the kind of saint that Valjean finally becomes. The universal aspect of *Les Misérables* has less to do with political upheaval or revolution than with the eternal truths about human nature and our belief in God. In essence, the story of Jean Valjean is that of a sudden Pauline conversion, and a determination to retain the almost impossible ethical standards he has set himself. The quest for saintliness is the one thing that all religions have in common.'

Roger Allam, Colm Wilkinson, Michael Ball, Frances Ruffelle and the original Barbican and Palace cast of *Les Misérables* at the very beginning of a triumphant revolution.

10

THE MAN
IN THE MASK

"The magic of the music of the night"

'The general consensus was that Café Puccini, not Phantom, was going to be an enormous hit'

Concurrently with Cameron's production of *Les Mis*, he was also talking with Andrew about a new show. Tim Rice had temporarily lost interest in the musical theatre after their one mutual flop (*Blondel*), but Lloyd Webber, hard at work on a requiem in memory of his father with his wife, Sarah Brightman, as soloist, was keen to embark on a major new show.

One day, early in their marriage, she had been asked to audition for Ken Hill's new version of the gothic melodrama, *The Phantom of the Opera*. Although she had no hesitation in turning down the low-budget production, the idea now occurred to Andrew that a broad-stage musical version, cutting and pasting out-of-copyright operatic arias of the old Gaston Leroux chiller might be a fun project for him to produce with Cameron. Cameron was wildly enthusiastic but was surprised that Andrew didn't seem at the time to want to compose an original score. Andrew said that the original story contained operatic excerpts, and he didn't again want to be accused of writing pastiche.

Ken Hill's show, without Sarah, was mounted at the Theatre Royal, Stratford East, and one evening Cameron (with Michael) and Andrew (with Sarah) went to see it. They liked what they saw and spent the next month meeting with Ken Hill to try to work out a way to expand his show into a West End musical. At the end of this period they decided, mutually, that the show they had seen was not, in fact, one that needed or wanted expansion. On the contrary, there was room for another kind of *Phantom*, just as there had always been room for another film version. Andrew and Cameron decided to pursue the plot with existing music from the period. They watched all the film versions and promptly decided to go back to the original novel, which was long out of print.

The first director they approached to talk about it was Jim Sharman, of the original *Superstar* and *Rocky Horror Show*. On a trip to Japan they all discussed it at length and it was Sharman who told them that the project would be more attractive with an original Lloyd Webber score. Andrew didn't respond immediately but, back in England at Sydmonton, he invited Cameron for a drink and told him he had decided to write it himself, adding that the extraordinary range of Sarah's voice had finally revealed to him the key to both the score and, indeed, the central character of Christine. Andrew also knew (though he seldom cared to admit it) that without Cameron there would have been no *Cats* and now, albeit for the last time, he decided that he wanted to go back to that triumphant partnership.

On the face of it, they were starting out on much safer territory. Unlike *Cats*, *The Phantom of the Opera* had been around in the public consciousness for almost a century: first of all in the original Gaston Leroux thriller (published 1911), then in countless silent and sound movies, the most famous of which starred Lon Chaney (1925 silent), Claude Rains (1943) and Herbert Lom (1962). Then there were several television versions, including the 1983 Maximilian Schell version as well as, in the same year, a satirical rock opera by Brian de Palma called *The Phantom of the Paradise*. Even while Hal Prince and Lloyd Webber were in rehearsal in 1986, yet another stage musical *Phantom* was being tried out off-Broadway, while the original trigger of Lloyd Webber's interest in the project,

WYNDHAM'S
Ω THEATRE
Ian B. Albery · Managing Director
Charing Cross Road · London WC2

Ken Hill's Stratford East musical, was touring the UK. And all of these were based on the story of the ugly genius falling hopelessly in love with an opera singer but unable to express himself except through music. It could even be argued that *The Phantom of the Opera* was little more than a rethink of three other Victorian horror classics: Bram Stoker's *Dracula*, Mary Shelley's *Frankenstein* and Robert Louis Stevenson's *Dr Jekyll and Mr Hyde*.

Having realigned himself with Cameron, another idea of Andrew's surfaced. For several years he had wanted to write a musical life of Puccini, the operatic composer he most admired. They went to the broadcaster and musicologist Robin Ray to write the book. What resulted was *Café Puccini*, devised by Ray, with whom Cameron had worked so happily on *Tomfoolery* a few years earlier. It was in fact a play with music, and it was an attempt to tell the story of the great composer's uneasy life within the framework of his greatest hits. In a way, it was to be another celebration cabaret, but this time with a plot. Thus the first half of the evening sounded like an unusually jovial Radio Three documentary but when, after the interval, the show moved into the darkness of Puccini's tortured marriage and the awful affair of the maid driven to suicide by a wife who on this one occasion had misjudged her husband's infidelity, it became something of a mess. But Ray was lucky in his casting: Nicola McAuliffe was a wonderful double as wife and mother, Lewis Fiander was a suitably bemused Puccini and William Blezard led a jaded band in the style of Puccini's own café arrangements.

Café Puccini closed abruptly at Wyndham's in less than a month, after some appalling reviews. It was to be Cameron's last flop for seven years, and the last time, until *Moby Dick*, that he would bring to London a show which clearly didn't have the strength to survive there.

Ironically, at the previous summer's

1986 – Robin Ray's short-lived attempt to tell the story of Giacomo Puccini's complex love life against the background of his own music starred Lewis Fiander and Nicola McAuliffe.

Sydmonton Festival, where traditionally Andrew has always premièred his new scores in the little church in his garden, both *Café Puccini* and *The Phantom of the Opera* were given their first stagings. At lunch afterwards the general consensus was that *Café Puccini* was going to be an enormous hit with immediate offers for both West End and Broadway, but *The Phantom of the Opera* didn't stand a ghost of a chance.

While Andrew was busy making a Ken Russell video for the title song, with lyrics by Mike Batt (who also produced the single), Cameron was once again searching for lyricists. The first person he approached was Tom Stoppard, who had just completed a new version of Prokofiev's *The Love of Three Oranges* for the English National Opera. Tom quickly returned the novel with a sharp letter saying that had Andrew Lloyd Webber's name not been attached to the project he would never have reached the end of such a rubbishy little novel. Cameron then suggested Herbert Kretzmer, but a relationship between Lloyd Webber's music and Kretzmer's lyrics was not a natural linking, and thirdly, the man whom of all living musical showmen Andrew most admired, Alan Jay Lerner. Over lunch Alan told Andrew three things – that the idea was brilliant, that he was flattered to be asked and that he had just been told he had less than three months to live.

Of the other possible candidates whom Andrew now had to approach, Tim Rice made it clear, particularly after their 'Memory' squabble, that he had no interest in rejoining his old partner; T. S. Eliot, being dead, was equally unavailable; Don Black and Alan Ayckbourn were reckoned altogether too contemporary for the project, and of his known colleagues that

left Andrew with Richard Stilgoe, the amiable comic pianist who had been ideal for the transference of *Starlight Express* from children's nursery story to rock–disco musical, and who had the inestimable advantage of being the fastest lyricist in the West.

Thus it was Stilgoe who, in the February of 1986, started to work on the words for what Andrew was now convinced would be his masterpiece and the final justification and apotheosis of his marriage to Sarah Two. But after the try-out at Sydmonton it was clear that although Stilgoe had the wit and the elegance required, he lacked the poetry and passion, and he was abruptly sidelined to 'Book and Additional Lyrics'. Cameron and Andrew started again on the search for a lyricist.

And it was Cameron who found him. The Vivian Ellis Awards every year give cash and encouragement to unknown British songwriters; at the 1986 ceremony, he heard the work of Charles Hart, one of that year's runners-up. Hart was barely twenty-five years old when he was asked by Mackintosh to submit some dummy lyrics to the *Phantom* score, without knowing who its composer was, to spare him unnecessary pressure. As a result it was he who was ultimately responsible for the words that go with the music of the night.

If one surprise was Andrew's choice of a new lyricist, the second and greater shock concerned his choice of director. Trevor Nunn, now free of the RSC, had directed not only Lloyd Webber's *Cats* and *Starlight Express* but also Boublil–Schönberg's *Les Misérables*; he was now also working with Tim Rice on the revamp of *Chess*, necessitated by the AIDS illness of Michael Bennett, the original director. Not surprisingly, therefore, he assumed he would also be asked back for *Phantom*. Not in fact. Backstage at that year's Tony Awards in New York, Andrew had run into an even earlier colleague, the American director Hal Prince, who had been so centrally a part of the success of *Evita*. 'What,' asked Andrew, 'are you doing now?' 'Looking,' replied Hal, 'for a really romantic musical.' 'I've got you one,' said Andrew, 'I'm going to do *The Phantom of the Opera*.' 'Partner,' said Hal, 'you've got it.'

But things are never quite that easy. Within three months, it became clear to Andrew and Cameron that Hal's recent string of New York musicals did not make him the golden boy of that particular moment. It was, as usual, Cameron who had to break the news to Prince that he was no longer on the team. Prince, with no contract yet negotiated, accepted the inevitable with his usual grace, thanked

Cameron for the introduction to designer Maria Björnson and disappeared into the night.

Andrew, once accused of discarding lyricists like Kleenex, now decided to return to Trevor Nunn. This also proved characteristically short-lived. After the opening of *Les Mis* Andrew decided that Trevor was also unsuited to the new project and with undue haste hurried back to Hal Prince, who felt himself now in a stronger position than he had been first time around.

With Hal finally on board, the rest of the artistic team was complete. Gillian Lynne of *Cats* was again to choreograph, and Andrew Bridge was to light Maria Björnson's stunning recreation of the Paris Opera House in one of the most lavish sets that the West End had seen since before the war, complete with crashing chandelier and candle-lit subterranean lake.

Except for Sarah Brightman, the other leading players in the Sydmonton try-out of *Phantom* were now all involved in the highly successful *Les Misérables*, which had opened several months earlier and were therefore unavailable for *Phantom*. Other Webber regulars such as David Essex and Paul Nicholas were clearly far too rock based for a score which was fractionally this side of grand opera. The solution ultimately came from neither Andrew nor Cameron, nor yet Hal Prince but Sarah herself, who happened to mention an actor with whom she shared a singing teacher. He was the forty-four-year-old Michael Dumble-Smith, who had already starred in such West End hits as *Billy* and *Barnum*, but was in fact best known for a long-running television sitcom called *Some Mothers Do 'Ave 'Em*. By then, of course, he had changed his name to Michael Crawford. Steve Barton, from the Vienna *Cats*, was cast in the third crucial role, that of Raoul, the Vicomte on whose memory the plot depends.

With the principals in place and the score almost complete, Cameron's next problem was where to put *Phantom*. Lloyd Webber's own

The Prince of Broadway – Hal Prince came in to direct *Phantom* with a lifetime of New York producing and directing experience; in musical terms he was far and away the most distinguished director Cameron or Andrew had ever worked with.

Costume designs by Maria Björnson for the original production of *Phantom* in London.

Palace was still selling out nightly, with *Les Misérables*. In any case, what they really wanted was a theatre with a strong sense of Victorian identity, and the only one of these to come free was Her Majesty's, which had recently seemed unlucky (not least because of the flop there of Lloyd Webber's original *Jeeves*) but had earlier been a long-run home for both *West Side Story* and *Fiddler on the Roof*. Moreover, it was sturdy enough to stand a chandelier crashing to the stage eight performances a week. Most importantly, all Sir Herbert Beerbohm Tree's original Victorian stage machinery remained intact, lacking only electrification. Its only drawback was a relatively small capacity of 1,200 seats, but the theatre's manager, Louis Benjamin, was so eager to have the show that

Cameron was able to obtain it for a remarkably low rental, one that he enjoys to this day.

As *Phantom* went into rehearsal, it became clear that despite its magical special effects, the show did not intend to bombard us with technology in the way that such forerunners as *Time* and Lloyd Webber's own *Starlight Express* had used gimmickry and gadgetry to conceal the lack of any real plot. This was, as Prince and Lloyd Webber kept emphasizing, to be a fundamentally romantic show. Lloyd Webber's already established passions for Victorian art and ecclesiastical architecture were beginning to spill over on to his stage.

For Hal Prince, the emotional breakthrough came when, by chance, he saw a BBC television documentary in which a number of

paraplegics and other severely disabled people talked about the ways in which deformity can be erotic. Hal realized then that he was indeed telling a love story, albeit a curiously obsessive and deformed one.

Talking years later to Carol Ilson, Prince remembered *Phantom* as one of the happiest theatrical times of his life. 'For a year prior to rehearsals we had worked very hard on the material...I kept flying to London to work with Andrew and his lyricist and designer or they came here...and then, about half-way through the process, we had actors sing it for us in Andrew's office and we saw what was wrong with it and then went on to the next step...We then went into rehearsals in a kind of recreation hall across the Thames in Lambeth in an atmosphere that was really lovely. I rehearsed every day from ten 'til one and then I would go home [leaving the company to rehearse]; almost everything is the way it was staged the first time. It was beautiful weather so I would walk around London, have dinner with friends,

'Phantom *was the first musical ever to star a falling chandelier*'

go to a theatre and then back to rehearsal next morning. After four weeks of that we were in the theatre and then we previewed and it was a smash...It was really no more difficult or dangerous than that. With Cameron there was none of the economic pressure that you get on

Leroux melodrama is in fact a marvellous celebration of its own theatrical surroundings. How delighted Beerbohm Tree, Her Majesty's first builder and manager almost a century ago and a man not above sticking live rabbits through the scenery of Shakespeare to hold audience

Far left – Michael Crawford and Sarah Brightman in Cameron Mackintosh's original production of *The Phantom of the Opera*.

Broadway, but England has always been a much healthier and sensible climate.'

After the traditional week of desperately shaky dress rehearsals *The Phantom of the Opera* opened on 9 October 1986 to a healthy £1 million advance, which just about paid for Maria Björnson's sets. The expert make-up artist, Chris Tucker, who had turned John Hurt into the Elephant Man, was brought in to achieve Crawford's stunning half-mask face, and Cameron had ensured that nowhere were short cuts taken in any area of a production everyone somehow just knew could not fail.

It occurred to many of us on that first night that the plot of *The Phantom of the Opera* is essentially simple enough: ghost gets girl, ghost loses girl. But the show built around the old

attention, would have been. He would have loved the gasps that came from the stalls as the chandelier rises to the roof, only to come crashing down again, or as the stage is magically transformed into the roof-tops of Paris or the candle-lit underground lake. The whole of this *Phantom* was a tribute to old Victorian theatrical values, almost as though Lloyd Webber wanted to reassure us that, after the chilly mechanics of *Starlight Express*, he was still capable of returning us to a world of lyrical romanticism, somewhere half-way from Ivor Novello back to Puccini.

Phantom was the first musical ever to star a falling chandelier; nothing else in the production was ever quite so dramatically effective or well lit, a tribute to the prescence of the

American actress and lyricist, Gretchen Cryer, whose fury at the original *Cats* had given rise to her fantasy that one day a show would be written about chandeliers. Well, here it was.

As the Phantom, Michael Crawford managed to be everywhere around the set, wreaking murder and mayhem on those who dared thwart his plans to make a star of his beloved Christine. Sarah Brightman had exactly the right kind of wide-eyed innocence for that role, but neither she nor Steve Barton as the Vicomte who also loves her, was ever given any but the most minimal characterization. In stripping away the minor themes and strands of the original Leroux, the production became a simple spectacular that could almost have been called *Beauty and the Beast,* an idea Disney got to only a decade later. But there were some marvellously magical moments in the Lloyd Webber creation, and if his Phantom was made out to be no more than a crazed subterranean organist in a half-mask, Michael Crawford yet managed to create of him a literally haunting figure.

Following the battle plan they had established five years earlier with *Cats,* as soon as *Phantom* was up and running at Her Majesty's, where it celebrated its eleventh birthday on 9 October 1997, Cameron and Andrew started to plan the Broadway transfer. But not without considerable difficulty. Two of the three stars had no problem with American Equity: Crawford had worked on Broadway before and was anyway given star status because of his appearance opposite Barbra Streisand in the movie *Hello Dolly!,* while Steve Barton, although long resident in Europe, was actually American born.

The problem was, quite simply, Sarah. Despite her considerable new-found fame in Britain, American Equity ruled that she was not 'a star of international standing' and refused to approve her entry visa. 'Why should we let her work here?' asked Alan Eisenberg, then Execu-

tive Secretary of American Actors' Equity, 'when there are so many young American actresses currently unemployed who could play that part just as well?' Urged on by Andrew, Hal Prince annouced that he would not open the show with any other actress and, for good measure, Lloyd Webber added, 'If Sarah doesn't go, the show doesn't go.'

A deal was finally brokered by which, in return for Sarah being allowed to play Broadway, Andrew promised to give at least one 'non-star' American a leading role in a new show of his within five years. This was a promise he duly kept with the casting of Ann Crumb in his *Aspects of Love*, though he may have come to regret when, having fallen on the set, Crumb sued him and the Really Useful Group, settling for an undisclosed but substantial sum of money, the first of many actresses to do so.

All other hurdles overcome, *The Phantom of the Opera* opened with its three original stars at the Majestic Theatre in New York on 26 January 1988 where, as of this writing, it still plays eight performances a week. Even before the first night

1996 – Andrew and Cameron (below) prepare to cut the cake which celebrated the tenth birthday of *The Phantom of the Opera* in London.

it had already broken all existing box-office records by taking an unprecedented advance of $16 million, thus rendering the usually powerful New York critics irrelevant.

Clive Barnes, the only Londoner to have survived as a critic on the Great White Way for almost half a century, opined that *Phantom* was 'the hottest thing to hit Broadway since the tip-up seat', but the natives were less welcoming, if not downright hostile. 'It is not so much,' wrote John Simon in *New York* magazine, 'that Lloyd Webber lacks an ear for melody as that he has too much of one for other people's melodies.' The large advance and overwhelming audience acceptance of the show defeated the notion that the *New York Times* and its former critic, Frank Rich, had the power to make or break a show. Rich found the lyrics 'numbing', the choreography 'repetitive' and the show 'a victory for dynamic stagecraft over musical kitsch'. Despite this and his highly personal attack on Sarah Brightman's looks, *The Phantom of the Opera* is still one of New York's triumphs.

A run of over ten years and seven Tony Awards should have been a consolation, but Lloyd Webber has never got over his feeling that Rich had been out to get his beloved Sarah, and Cameron has never since worked on a show with Andrew. As for the Brightman–Lloyd Webber marriage, that came to an end on 5 November 1990.

11

BROADWAY BABIES

"Good times and bum times,
I've seen them all and, my dear, I'm still here"

"There will always be people who prefer the original but I think our version worked better"

By now, Cameron's corner shop had become a worldwide chain of department stores. This would never have been possible without three crucial people. Martin McCallum set up the international network, organizing the many companies that now form the Mackintosh Office and helping Cameron to find the many talented people who share his dreams. Back home, Nick Allott, who had started out as the house manager of the New London theatre when *Cats* opened, was quickly promoted to run Cameron's British operation. And Tee Hesketh, who had retired from John Hallett's Associated Theatres, came out of retirement to become Cameron's indispensable personal assistant, in which capacity she continues to run his professional life. Also invaluable are Bob West, the supreme company manager, and Sue Ewings, the queen of the box-office. This core team are at the heart of an ever-expanding empire that allows Cameron to use his time to create new shows and sustain the vibrancy of the old ones.

Thanks to Andrew and Cameron and Tim Rice, the London theatre had discovered the joys of the mega-musical, some thirty years after they had first been seen in bulk on Broadway. Audiences now wanted to see how their ever-increasing ticket money was being spent, and small would not be beautiful again for some years. By 1984 ticket prices along Shaftesbury Avenue had climbed through the hitherto unthinkable £15 barrier. *Starlight Express,* the first of the new Lloyd Webbers not to involve Cameron, at a production cost of £2.5 million, set a new record in that year as the most expensive musical ever staged in

Britain. A scant dozen years later, tickets broke the stratospheric £35 watermark and costs were now proportionately higher.

By the summer of 1984, no less than twenty-two musicals, new and old, were playing in greater London at roughly one in every two theatres. That figure was to remain almost constant over the next decade, with only a slight rise in the number of non-Broadway and non-vintage shows.

While Cameron was waiting for the next Boublil–Schönberg, he turned back to Stephen Sondheim, the only living American composer with whom he had already forged a close relationship. The success of *Side by Side by*

1987 – The London première of *Follies,* coming after more than a decade after the Broadway original, was drastically revised by Stephen Sondheim and James Goldman to meet what Cameron felt were the demands of a British audience. The story was given a more up-beat ending, and the four London stars (Diana Rigg, Julia McKenzie, Daniel Massey and David Healy) were joined, as in New York, by a collection of showbiz veterans including Dolores Gray, Adele Leigh, Pearl Carr and Teddy Johnson. The Broadway Babes had never looked so good. *Follies* was at once the greatest celebration and the most heartfelt lament for a lost world of greasepaint and glamour that even Sondheim had ever achieved, and its score contains the anthems to suvival which lie at the heart of Cameron's theatrical philosophy.

120

Sondheim back in 1977 convinced them that they should work together again, and soon afterwards it became clear that Stephen's This was long overdue for a London première. This is the bitter-sweet account of a group of Ziegfeld Follies girls, some years past their prime, at a theatrical reunion.

'It was Julia McKenzie,' says Cameron, 'who first suggested doing Follies when we were in the middle of Side by Side by Sondheim, and I even talked to Trevor Nunn and Gillian Lynne about another partnership with the RSC after Les Mis. But that idea came to nothing and I soon realized that what I really wanted was a new version of the 1971 Broadway original, which I had found brilliant but very clinical. Somehow it refused to involve you in the story.'

As far as Sondheim was concerned, 'Oscar Hammerstein always taught me to be ruthless with material, so I had no problem in throwing out even my favourite song when Cameron said it got too gloomy too soon. James Goldman, who wrote the book, also now felt the need for change seventeen years on.'

For Cameron, 'There will always be people who prefer the original but I think our version worked better for an audience. That doesn't make it a better show, though; there is something fatally flawed about Follies which makes it very difficult to do. Like Pal Joey, everyone wants to have a go at it because you always think you can crack it, but there is something inherent that stops you ever getting it really right. All the same, I'm very proud to have done it and delighted that we ran almost two years, twice the original New York run.'

Follies always had a curious history; it began with Sondheim and Goldman seeing in the New York Times the photograph of an ancient Gloria Swanson standing amid the bulldozed rubble of a theatre where she had first been a dancer more than fifty years earlier. The show they created had run an acceptable 522 performances on Broadway and won several Tony Awards for a vintage cast led by Alexis Smith, Gene Nelson and Yvonne de Carlo. Yet both Sondheim and his first choreographer, Michael Bennett, thought there was something wrong with the book. It wasn't until an amazing *Follies in Concert* revival for two nights at Lincoln Center in 1985 (this time the all-stars included Barbara Cook, Elaine Stritch, Carol Burnett, Lee Remick, Betty Comden and Adolph Green) that the show really came into its own. It was then that the London production became a real project for Cameron, although the show had

designed by Maria Björnson, which threatened to be more eventful than the plot, the director Mike Ockrent had to find some West End equivalents to the original American mix of ancient Broadway and Hollywood legends.

The central casting for London featured Diana Rigg and the late Daniel Massey as the wealthy, clenched, up-market couple with Julia

already been seen elsewhere in Britain, notably at Wythenshawe and subsequently at Leicester, where Paul Kerryson runs a one-man campaign to ensure that Sondheim shows are lovingly mounted for British audiences.

Cameron chose the suitably grandiose and faintly seedy Shaftesbury Theatre for *Follies* where, on a set composed mainly of scaffolding

McKenzie and David Healy as the pair from the back of beyond; and the newly written ending allowed them to avoid nervous collapse while staying within rocky marriages. The rest of an amazing company of forty included Dolores Gray (followed by Eartha Kitt) for 'I'm Still Here'; Margaret Courtenay belting out the first big hit of the evening, perhaps not so

much a Broadway as a Broadstairs Baby; Pearl Carr and Teddy Johnson from seaside singalongs with 'Rain on the Roof'; and Maria Charles from *The Boy Friend* with 'Ah, Paree'. They also got Adele Leigh from the Vienna Woods with 'One Last Kiss', and Leonard Sachs from 'The Good Old Days' was the Mr Producer who gave both the party and the title to this book.

But, although Sondheim had written four new songs for the London première, some seemed to belong in his *Company*, while none solved the great difficulty of the second half, which is that Goldman's plot still runs out at the interval. Up to there, what we have is musically and architecturally a fascinating folly about the schizoid nature of nostalgia. If you can imagine a stage spectacular cobbled together on a wet afternoon by Proust and Pirandello, with a little help from the Berlins, Irving and Isaiah, you'll have some idea of the scale on which *Follies* has been conceived. Old ladies are shadowed on-stage by the ghostly dancers they once were, surrounded by one of the most brilliant scores that even Sondheim ever devised, one that manages to recall three entire generations of Broadway shows, while simultaneously celebrating and mocking the very essence of them. *Follies* may be a flawed masterpiece, but it remains musically and lyrically one of the richest of all Sondheim treats.

12

FROM PINKERTON TO PRYCE

"The heat is on in Saigon"

"By the end of the evening there was no choice to be made. I had to produce Miss Saigon"

ameron always said that when the suggestion of *Les Misérables* first came up he had never even read the novel. By the time of *Miss Saigon*, four years later, he had at least been to see its acknowledged source, which was Puccini's opera *Madama Butterfly*.

'I first got to hear about this musical in the foyer of the Palace Theatre on Wednesday 4 December 1985, during the party following the first performance of the angst-filled transfer of *Les Misérables* from the Barbican Theatre. Alain, Claude-Michel and I heaved a collective sigh of relief, and during the evening they cornered me, asking nervously if they now had a profession as writers of musicals. I told them they had, and they said, "Good, we want to start on our next idea." Having piqued my interest they then absolutely refused to tell me anything more about the project, not even its name. The more impatient I became at their silence, the more they enjoyed teasing me. Then one day in May 1986 Alain called and said could Claude-Michel and he come round for dinner so they could play me the first act. Alain told me they were calling the show *Miss Saigon*. The score had a drive and restless energy which was as modern as any I have ever heard in a contemporary musical. By the end of the evening there was no choice to be made. I had to produce *Miss Saigon*.

'Now I was hooked, the journey to Saigon was beginning in earnest. My initial reaction to the show was that it was a restless, dangerous musical – its score reflecting the bottled up tension of those last dark days in Vietnam. Those first impressions of the score gave me two pointers. One, that the show should be a completely different animal from *Les Misérables*, with a different look and style and a strong element of movement (not dance) to complement the restless score.

'Second, its subject matter made me feel this could be the first musical I could seriously contemplate premièring in America. Though the musical is not about Vietnam, its story is tragically so plausible and appears in so many similar guises in the media, day after day, we knew that every element of the musical had to be a theatrical distillation of reality. Alain and Claude-Michel had written a tragic musical love story, not a musical comedy.'

Cameron understands exactly what the process is for Boublil and Schönberg, and that they can't be rushed. 'What one has to understand about Claude-Michel and Alain is that the most difficult thing for them is to find a subject. Once they have, they spend the next six months giving each other reasons not to do it. Then, when they have run out of those reasons, they get to work. Another three months they then spend writing the scenario, without a word of lyric or a note of music, until they achieve a story in which the mood, the tension and the dramatic cohesion is complete. Once they are duly imbued with exactly the same material, they go off separately to write the music and lyrics, but they have already had all the arguments.

'That's when I come in, when they have already been at work for at least a year and the construction is complete. Producers and directors should never write themselves; we are there to complement the writers' imagination and to bring the writing to its best fruition. What I am very good at is saying when bits of

The original press photograph which inspired *Miss Saigon*.

famous photograph of Gloria Swanson, so *Miss Saigon* started with Schönberg finding in a French magazine a news shot of a Vietnamese mother handing over her child to an American soldier at the airport in Saigon.

'I had no idea,' said Schönberg, 'how important that photograph would be for me...the silence of this woman, stunned by her grief, was a shout of pain louder than any of the earth's laments. The child's tears were the final condemnation of all wars which shatter people who love each other. The little Vietnamese girl was about to board a plane for the United States where her father, an ex-GI she had never seen, was waiting for her. Her mother was leaving her there and would never see her again...She knew, as only a woman could, that beyond this departure gate there was both a new life for her daughter and no life at all for her and yet she had willed it.'

Very early in their discussions it became clear to both Boublil and Schönberg that what they had here was a Vietnam update on *Madama Butterfly*, as Alain explains. 'We saw *Miss Saigon* as our own story, but retaining the basic *Butterfly* plot of a misunderstanding between two individuals of highly different cultures, at a time when that misunderstanding could also reflect a much deeper one between two countries at war.'

While this was, on the surface, a less immediately French project for the two Frenchmen than *Les Misérables*, or their original *La Revolution Française*, it is worth remembering that Vietnam, like Boublil's native Tunisia, had been under French control and was centrally part of the French colonial experience. They began reading extensively around the subject

the script are dull or a song doesn't reach a proper climax. For example, at the beginning of *Miss Saigon*, Chris, the GI who falls in love with Kim, cries, "Why, God, why?" about the war. That is his major crisis and we have to understand his state of mind for Vietnam and this love affair to have such a dramatic effect on him. That first song was not in the original score; we hammered it out between us, they wrote it, but when it wasn't right or disturbing enough I nagged on. I do that a lot with orchestrations too. I need to feel this or that and I know when the audience just won't get it. If we are not getting the most out of a scene I just keep on and on until, if only to shut me up, they go away and at least think about it again. I rarely, if ever, come up with the perfect solution; but I am nearly always spot on about the areas that are weak and need rethinking. I constantly prod all my creative and backstage people to go away and re-examine and find something to make me shut up. That is what I do best.'

Just as *Follies* had been inspired by that

of the war, on one occasion coming up with a French magazine article describing a Thai-based adventurer known as 'L'Ingénieur'. Thus was born the Engineer, the amoral Eurasian 'fixer', whose commercial exploitations bring the characters of *Miss Saigon* together.

In its final form *Miss Saigon* is as close to *Madama Butterfly* as *West Side Story* is to

had done an extensive rewrite virtually from the ground up. Besides, I am not a political writer; I'm a South African resident in London and I told them that what they needed was an American lyric writer who would not have to reach for the idiom.'

By now this had also occurred to Cameron, and he had therefore approached Richard

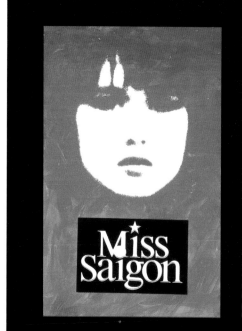   

Romeo and Juliet. And, like *West Side Story*, *Miss Saigon* was to pass through several pairs of hands before it reached its final form. Both Boublil and Schönberg speak good English but, naturally, not quite good enough for solo lyric writing, which requires a native speaker to capture nuance and mood, so the first draft of the songs was in French. It was therefore back to Herbert Kretzmer, who had written the triumphant English lyrics for *Les Misérables*, that they first went to discuss the anglicizing of *Miss Saigon*.

'But it was clear,' says Kretzmer, 'that this time Alain wanted to write it all himself with just a little help on areas he was finding difficult. It wouldn't be at all like *Les Mis* where I

Maltby, with whom he had happily worked on the Broadway revisions to Lloyd Webber's *Song and Dance*. At first, Maltby turned them down on the grounds that by 1986 the last thing Americans wanted was a show reminding them of the first war they had ever lost, but the more he heard of the score the more he realized that he had to be involved. 'At first,' says Maltby, 'we weren't doing lyrics at all. We started out writing a play, developing the characters and the drama in a language far removed from conventional musicals and only at the end of that long process did the dialogue start to turn into lyrics.'

From this time forward, Cameron almost always tried to match a new musical to a new directing talent and, after considerable debate, he decided that the man for *Miss Saigon* was to be Nicholas Hytner, whom he had long admired. At this time, long before *The Madness of King George III* was on stage or screen, Hytner, just thirty, was best known for some classical hits at the Royal Exchange, Manchester, and the RSC. He had, however, also done

decided on an American director he went to Jerome Robbins, who turned him down. There was then a period of flux, lasting about a year, while Jerry Zaks was at the helm, but when no Broadway theatre of the right size was available and David Merrick finally decided to close *42nd Street* at Drury Lane, Zaks said he did not want to come to London to work for a

1989 – The making of another masterpiece. Early poster designs for *Miss Saigon* by Dewynters.

one *Don Carlos* and a National Theatre staging of *Ghetto*, a play which involved the singing by Maria Friedman of several Jewish traditional songs. He was, in that sense, an even braver choice than Trevor Nunn had been for *Les Mis*, but by now Cameron was confident enough in his own judgement to prefer shows on which he could leave his producer's mark at least as clearly and firmly as that of any director. From now on, whatever the casting and whoever the creative team, these would henceforth always be truly the musicals of Cameron Mackintosh.

Because of its centrally American subject matter, Cameron's original plan was to open the show in the United States. He had first spoken with Trevor Nunn, but when he

number of reasons, including his children's school holidays.

In this long four-year period of pre-production, Trevor Nunn was courting Andrew Lloyd Webber, who initially wanted Nicholas Hytner to direct *Aspects of Love*. But Hytner's commitment to *Ghetto* at the National Theatre could not be moved to accommodate Lloyd Webber's schedule, so Andrew went to Nunn. Trevor still wanted to do *Miss Saigon* but Cameron became convinced that he was simply not right for the material. Once Trevor had committed to *Aspects of Love*, Cameron quickly persuaded Hytner to direct *Miss Saigon*. Trevor was deeply disappointed at Cameron's decision, and it was then to be several years before

Left – Jonathan Pryce as the original Engineer in *Miss Saigon*, a performance he almost didn't get to repeat on Broadway.

"Surely you do not wish to call the show Miss Saigon? The correct title is of course Miss Ho Chi Minh City"

Above left – The original Broadway stars, Willy Falk and Lea Salonga. Above right – Cameron with Lea Salonga (right) and Monique Wilson (left).

the two old friends and colleagues spoke to each other again.

Hytner, for his part, was taking on not just his first major commercial assignment at the end of a long line of infinitely more established directors, but was also required to adopt a production team which had been in place now for many months. Apart from Mackintosh, Boublil, Schönberg and Maltby, this also included Bob Avian, Michael Bennett's long-time assistant, who had been Cameron's choreographer on the London *Follies*, and also the *Cats–Les Mis* team of John Napier (designer), David Hersey (lighting), Andrew Bruce (sound) and several others. So, by the late spring of 1989, already four years since the idea had first arisen, *Miss Saigon* was ready for the long and difficult process of casting.

For a neophyte director, accustomed to the

cloistered atmosphere of the RSC and the National, this must have been a fearsome project. It was, after all, more complicated than anything even Cameron had yet attempted, not least because, with the exception of the American contingent and the Eurasian Engineer, the rest of the cast is Asian. As regards the Engineer, Hytner and Mackintosh now took a decision which, although uncontroversial in London, was to lead them later into considerable trouble on Broadway. They cast Jonathan Pryce, a British stage and screen star who, although he had sung occasionally in public, notably in the 1971 *Caucasian Chalk Circle*, was now to take on his first major musical.

The rest of the casting was to prove infinitely more elusive. First, Mackintosh and Nick Allott scoured London to no avail, even asking the help of the Vietnamese Embassy. 'Surely,' they wrote back to Allott, 'you do not wish to call the show *Miss Saigon*? The correct title is of course *Miss Ho Chi Minh City*.'

The team quickly gave up on finding British Asians, though they did set up a training school for future cast replacements. They now went on a tour of the Pacific Rim, holding mass auditions wherever they went, from Hawaii to the Philippines to Hong Kong to the United States. They auditioned Chinese, Japanese, Filipinos, Americans of all colours and creeds, and even a few genuine Vietnamese. It was a long, hard, slow process.

Finally, the breakthrough occurred. In the Philippines they found a seventeen-year-old girl, Lea Salonga, who not only had the fragile beauty of a barely pubescent teenager, but also had the stage experience of a child star who had started in rock concerts at the age of

130

nine and gone on to extensive film and television roles in her native Manila. Indeed, what broke the casting deadlock had been the discovery of an amazingly professional Filipino repertory company, where all the great Broadway musicals from *Oklahoma!* to *La Cage aux Folles* were regularly staged. Cameron and his team found not only their first cast in those ranks but also several alternative casts, many of whom are still performing the show around the world ten years after its original premières. It remains, even today, the major source of Asian casts.

Before a single performance had been given anywhere in the world, *Miss Saigon* had already racked up production costs of £3.6 million and, just as there had been several nay-sayers who doubted the wisdom of musicals about dancing cats or revolting French peasants, there were a good many more who, like Richard Maltby, wondered whether a sing-along about Saigon would really make any box-office sense.

For Cameron, still working out of a cramped Bloomsbury office, there was one crucial difference this time. His *Cats* had already grossed more than £500 million worldwide and was now playing in twenty countries – in London alone it was making an annual profit of £1.7 million. He also had *Les Misérables* running in twelve countries for a gross of £200 million, £2.5 million of which was coming in from London alone, while *The Phantom of the Opera*, playing then – as now – in a much smaller theatre, was making £1 million a year at Her Majesty's. Whatever happened to *Miss Saigon*, Mackintosh wasn't about to starve. Indeed, by now he already had the house in Regent's Park, an inherited croft in Scotland, the cottage in Hampshire and the farmhouse in the south of France which have been his homes almost ever since. And he was still just forty-two.

All the same, there was a lot riding on this one. 'I know,' he told *Newsweek* just before *Miss Saigon* opened at the Theatre Royal, Drury Lane, on 20 September 1989, 'that I've already had three mega-hits in a row and as that is so unusual I'm totally resigned to having no more success. If, God forbid, *Miss Saigon* goes down the tube, I shall be disappointed, but no more, because I know I have already had more than my fair share.'

But, as ever, he wasn't leaving anything to chance. Having decided to go for broke, with lavish sets on a scale rarely if ever before seen on an English stage, he had also chosen to mount the show at the Theatre Royal, Drury Lane. This had always been his spiritual home since he had started there as a stagehand, and it was clearly the great crucible of the musical theatre on this side of the Atlantic since it was where all the major Rodgers–Hammerstein and Lerner–Loewe shows had played in his childhood.

'The moment I took Drury Lane I knew we had to do something with *Miss Saigon* that was quite different from what we might have done had we been at the Adelphi or the New

Cameron with one of the greatest of all Broadway choreographers, Bob Avian, during rehearsals for *Miss Saigon*. They also worked together on *Follies* and *Martin Guerre*.

London. The history of Drury Lane is the history of spectacle, and with John Napier's sets we purposely built a show which could actually overpower that stage. There has never been another production of *Miss Saigon* on quite the same scale, and not since *My Fair Lady* back in 1956 has a show truly filled that stage or had the same success.'

What he was referring to was the sheer scale of the production. Napier designed not only the interior of Saigon's houses and night-clubs, but also its exterior, culminating in a real helicopter that lifts off the roof of the American Embassy in Saigon eight times a week and twice on Wednesdays and Saturdays.

London rehearsals were complicated by the ambitious electronics of the set, which were apt to malfunction, causing on one occasion a near-death experience when a bit of scenery fell too near Lea Salonga, a redoubtable trouper who became famous backstage for her oft-repeated catchphrase, 'No problem'. Whatever was asked of her, no matter how dangerous or complex, her response was invariably, 'No problem', although as technical rehearsals proceeded she was beginning to worry about a gun in the second half which consistently misfired. But when, just before opening, part of the giant statue of Ho Chi Minh slipped its safety line and threatened to crush her and several others during a dress rehearsal, Cameron rushed backstage expecting to find his new star in a state of total collapse. 'No problem,' she insisted. 'Gun fired fine tonight.'

Six months before opening, Cameron had launched a £300,000 British advertising campaign, which he continued even when seats began to sell out, 'That,' he explained, 'is the best time to beat the drum – when people can't buy tickets you have to let them know what they are missing. That's the difference between a hit and a mega-hit.'

Right up to the first night, Mackintosh was still taking nothing for granted; in those last few days he had a high-profile row with the theatre's owners about the high selling price of their programmes, and refused to allow them to use his logo or sell his merchandise in the theatre. Instead, he set up a shop opposite the Lane to sell items such as mugs and T-shirts. He even appeared in person, working the queues for previews, distributing his free cast lists and gleefully demonstrating that in any battle with theatre managements Cameron Mackintosh was now the stronger – since an argument with him meant the theatre lost the revenue on the programmes and merchandise that they had historically considered their due. Never one to hold a grudge, he made it up with them and now they happily sell his merchandise on his terms.

Cameron managed also to announce two promenade matinees with the tickets at dramatically cut prices on the door so that, as he put it, 'Real theatregoers instead of just the very rich and far-sighted could get an early glimpse of the wonders of *Miss Saigon.*' Not since the heyday of David Merrick had there been such a showman.

The reviews for *Miss Saigon* at Drury Lane were vastly better than for any of Cameron's previous shows. True, the *Daily Express* complained, 'No real tunes here, despite snatches of melody in the ballads'; and for the *Daily Telegraph* Charles Osborne thought the show '…a cynically concocted product'. But both the *Daily Mail* and the *Financial Times* delivered raves, as did Michael Billington in the *Guardian*, '…an unusually intelligent and impassioned piece of popular theatre – revamped Puccini but with a sharp political edge. Here is a musical that addresses a modern tragedy with seriousness and integrity – it is rare and refreshing to find popular theatre that relates the personal to the political.' The Sunday papers were even better. It

133

132

did not take long for perceptive critics on both sides of the Atlantic to work out the pattern which linked all of Cameron's hits. *Cats* and *Les Mis* and *Phantom* and now *Miss Saigon* were all based on something mythic, something so central to human nature that they were at the same time universal and yet personal to every audience they played. All that remained now was to get *Miss Saigon* to Broadway and sort out the countless other overseas productions which would be well under way by the end of the first year.

During those first few months at Drury Lane new scenes and even a new ending were developed in time for the Broadway opening. This, however, was to prove vastly more tempestuous and controversial than anyone at the outset could have imagined. It all began months before the Broadway première, with a lobby of Asian–American actors objecting to the fact that Cameron had, from the very beginning, announced that Jonathan Pryce would play the leading role of the Engineer in New York, as well as in London. This faith was clearly justified by the performance itself, and the reviews for the Drury Lane opening were universally raves for Jonathan Pryce, who brought to the role a danger and sense of detail for which his career as a classical actor had uniquely prepared him. As it turned out, he could even sing splendidly.

The Asian–Americans demanded that their Equity should make it a condition of the Broadway opening that the role should go to one of them, and for months Mackintosh was locked, not for the last time, in an Equity battle which effectively rewrote Broadway history. The crisis came to a head in July 1990

when the leading American actress, Colleen Dewhurst, president of American Equity and B. D. Wong, the Chinese–American star of *M. Butterfly* announced that the granting of a visa to Pryce would send '...a dangerous and detrimental racial message...At this time in history, if black-face is wrong, so is yellow-face.' In private, Wong was even more forceful, telling his fellow actors, 'We may never be able to do the real work we dream of, if a Caucasian actor with taped eyelids is allowed to hop on Concorde...Chances to nail the big guys like this don't come often – let's go for it.'

Another Equity member claimed that Pryce came on-stage at Drury Lane '...painted yellow with taped slit eyes, fake bushy eyebrows and a wig.' In fact, Pryce had experi-

Miss Saigon – The Boublil–Schönberg update of *Madama Butterfly*, a musical which continues to sell out around the world. The power and the heartbreak of a child torn from its Vietnamese mother by an American father continues to find resonance in every country where it plays.

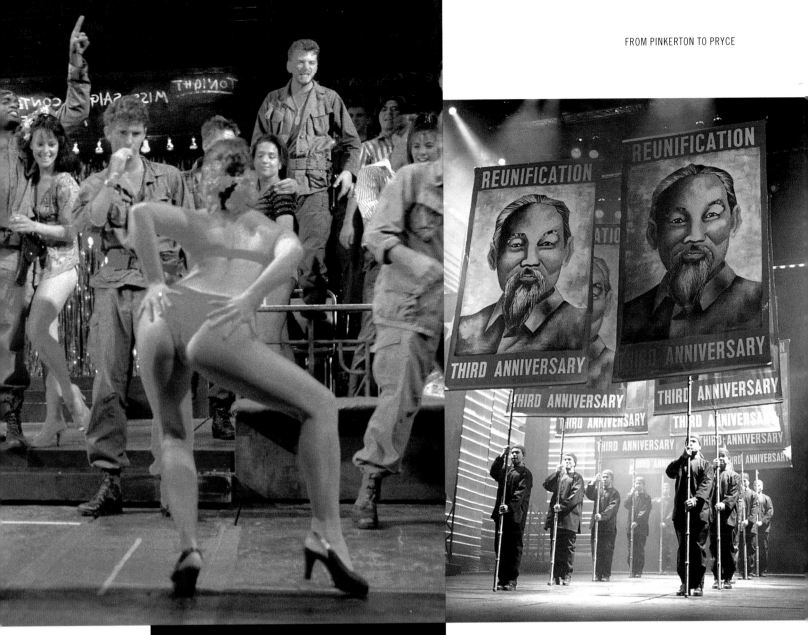

mented with make-up during rehearsals in an effort to emphasize the Asian side of his Eurasian character, but had come to the same conclusion as his New York colleagues. By the time he opened, he had long since ceased to tape his eyes, and abandoned any overtly Asian make-up.

To add insult to insult, Dewhurst, who ought to have known better, asked Cameron why, with a $25 million advance, he would care which actor played the Engineer. Battle was now joined and all through August messages flew across the Atlantic. Equity denied Pryce permission to take up his role, saying that after a long and emotional debate, it '…could not condone the casting of a Caucasian actor in the role of a Eurasian, as this is an affront to

Miss Saigon
CANCELLED

Actors' Equity has refused to approve Jonathan Pryce to play the role of the Engineer in the Broadway production of MISS SAIGON, as they cannot "condone the casting of a Caucasian actor in the role of a Eurasian." The creative team of MISS SAIGON finds this position to be irresponsible, and a disturbing violation of the principles of artistic integrity and freedom.

As a result, we are forced to announce the cancellation of next year's Broadway production of MISS SAIGON.

The debate is no longer about the casting of MISS SAIGON, but the art of acting itself. Because we feel so strongly about our own artistic position, we understand the depth of feeling within the Asian acting community and believe we share many of their aims. We passionately disapprove of stereotype casting, which is why we continue to champion freedom of artistic choice. Racial barriers can only undermine the very foundations of our profession.

We share the disappointment of the American public who have ordered tickets to see MISS SAIGON, but we look forward to a time when a calmer, more balanced atmosphere prevails.

The original British Company is currently running at The Theatre Royal, Drury Lane, London.

The Asian Company premieres at The Imperial Theatre, Tokyo on April 22, 1992 (Japanese language production).

INDIVIDUAL ORDERS

If you have received your tickets: Please return them, by mail, to Miss Saigon Refunds, P.O. Box 993, New York, NY 10108. Either a check will be mailed to you or a credit will be issued to your credit card account. **A refund cannot be issued unless tickets are returned.**

GROUP ORDERS
Please contact your Group Sales Agent for refund information.

9 August 1990 – The announcement in the *New York Times* that Cameron had decided to cancel the Broadway *Miss Saigon* in view of American Equity's refusal to allow Jonathan Pryce to play his original role. Equity soon relented, however, and the show went ahead as planned, opening at the Broadway Theatre in April 1991 where it continues to sell out to this day.

our Asian community.' However, in a curious footnote, Equity suggested that Mackintosh and Pryce '...might like to go for arbitration'. Mackintosh was not prepared even to do that , although it was clear that he would have won simply because of the large number of Equity members on- and backstage to whom he was giving employment, not only potentially in *Miss Saigon* but concurrently in his three other Broadway hits.

Instead, Mackintosh went on the counter-attack, announcing in the *New York Times* that he had cancelled the Broadway *Miss Saigon*, whose advance had now risen to a record-breaking $35 million, because 'We find the Equity decision a disturbing violation of the principles of artistic integrity and freedom and acting itself...The inaccurate and inflammatory statements made by Equity concerning *Miss Saigon* have only served to create a poisonous atmosphere in which artistic freedom cannot function or survive. Racial prejudice has triumphed over creative freedom and this is a sad reflection on the current state of the arts in America.'

He also pointed out that Asian–American actors, for whom there is rarely work on the New York stage, particularly on Broadway, would, without the Engineer, lose no fewer than thirty-six roles in *Miss Saigon*, and that many if not most of these actors would now miss making their Broadway debuts. And, he added, had the show been a success it would have provided employment for countless other Asian performers and an invaluable training ground for Asian–Americans.

To this day Cameron maintains that his decision to cancel was an absolutely genuine one, but he must have realized that Broadway could not afford to give *Miss Saigon* a miss. Within hours of the *New York Times* statement he found allies in the former New York, mayor Ed Koch, and the then drama critic of the *New York Times*, Frank Rich, who wrote that 'by barring Pryce under the disingenuous guise of promoting democracy, American Equity has stumbled into its very own Vietnam.'

Further support came from such prominent Equity members as John Malkovich and Charlton Heston, and very soon members from all over the country were demanding another special meeting. This one ended still more bizarrely with Colleen Dewhurst repeating all her original charges, including her description of *Miss Saigon* as 'a minstrel show', but ending, 'nevertheless we welcome Jonathan Pryce and wish Cameron Mackintosh's production a long and prosperous run in our country.'

Cameron was still not happy. The abrupt change of position by Equity was, he said, very welcome, but he must now have a guarantee that the union would not allow any of its members to continue the campaign. This was finally achieved in October 1990 when auditions for the Broadway *Miss Saigon* were resumed with a simple press ad reading 'The Heat is Back On'.

As the musical historian and critic Mark Steyn has noted, 'The irony of the whole situation was not lost on the production team; there would have been no *Miss Saigon* without the Vietnam War and its many social and psychological repercussions. But now, in turn, *Miss Saigon* itself had become a political issue in America, the controversy surrounding it provoking dramatic confrontation in a country profoundly altered by the fall of Saigon. To the bewilderment of its creators, what had begun as a show now became a landmark in the multi-racial history of a changing, post-Vietnam America. The experience gave special significance to the haunting cry that is both a recurring melody of *Miss Saigon*, its final heartbreaking lament, and its unanswerable question, "How, in one night, have we come so far?"'

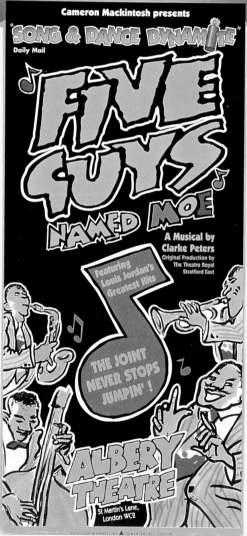

13

THE AMERICAN DREAM

"Ain't nobody here but us chickens"

❝Jolliness is all I want – everyone has to have a good time or else there is really no point in doing all this❞

With the Broadway opening of *Miss Saigon* in April 1991 Cameron Mackintosh, still only forty-five years old, had already staged more musicals in more cities than anyone else in theatre history. But he was not without his detractors. Back in London the judges of the Olivier Awards for that year, asked to name the best musical in the West End, chose not *Miss Saigon* but *Return to the Forbidden Planet*, a successful if somewhat shambolic rock version of Shakespeare's *The Tempest*, containing no original music at all. Their decision seemed to many a direct and hurtful insult. To Cameron it was simply confirmation of his belief in the idiocy of awards and it was but small satisfaction that, for the following year, the Olivier committee realigned not just its judges but also its categories.

Mackintosh, a pragmatic Scot who has always believed that his good fortune cannot last forever, was content in this particular year to note that he had already amassed a fortune of more than £200 million, thereby making him, according to *The Sunday Times*, the thirty-ninth richest man in Britain, with an annual income in the region of £7 million. Yet he has always maintained a comparatively simple lifestyle in which money itself, while pleasant, is very far from everything.

'I don't actually think about money at all – I just know I have got more than I can ever spend, but I still lead as normal a life as I can. I think you lose something if you don't ever have to queue. If you live only in a world where you just meet lovely people in private air terminals, you lose all sense of reality.' And, he might have added, you are also in danger of

losing touch with your audience, a loss of which he can never be accused.

His philosophy, whether for his audiences or his office workers, his backstage crews or his stars around the world, his family or indeed his few close friends, has always been very simple. 'Jolliness is really all I want – everyone has to have a good time or else there is really no point in doing all this. I was very hurt when Equity in America tried to make me out as a racist and I was disappointed and amazed when *Miss Saigon* got beaten by *Forbidden Planet* in the Oliviers, but at the end of the day there is really no point in dwelling on things like that.'

By the time it was ready for Broadway, *Miss Saigon* had become, at $11 million, the most expensive show in musical history and top tickets were selling for an all-time high of $100. But the show was fraught with danger: an incredibly complex set; the fear of first-night

1991 – Jonathan Pryce as the Engineer, Lea Salonga as Miss Saigon and Willy Falk as her GI lover, as seen by Al Hirschfeld for the *New York Times*.

picketing by those still angry at the casting of Jonathan Pryce; and, perhaps above all, the sense that *Miss Saigon* was in some ways a very anti-American show (nowhere more than in the Engineer's attempted rape of a Cadillac car in his signature song 'The American Dream'). All these meant the distinct possibility of a sharp backlash.

But, as with the earlier controversy over Sarah Brightman in *The Phantom of the Opera*, American Equity was in no mood for a fight and to be out-of-step with public opinion, so the British invasion continued unchallenged. Some indication of this situation had already occurred shortly after the opening of *Cats* in London when David Merrick, until then the leading impresario of Broadway musicals in the 1960s and 1970s, offered Cameron a straight swap – he would take all American rights in *Cats* and in return give Mackintosh all British rights in *42nd Street*, one of the great traditional Broadway hits. In 1981 that must have seemed like a good deal; by 1991, however, *42nd Street* had earned just $10 million worldwide while *Cats* was already way over $100 million, then the most profitable show in theatrical history and still no end in sight.

But with the opening on Broadway of *Miss Saigon*, it was, in one sense, the end of an era. Throughout the 1990s Cameron continued to produce on both sides of the Atlantic, while Lloyd Webber proved equally prolific. Yet neither of them came up with a show that could rival the success of the 'Big Four', and it is still on *Cats*, *Les Mis*, *Phantom* and *Miss Saigon* that the two great theatrical fortunes of this century are built.

And yet, on Broadway at least, Mackintosh

remains an anomaly. His shows are never vehicles for single stars, and few of them have the traditional 'eleven o'clock song' which you are supposed to leave theatres humming. If you were even to try a definition of what Boublil–Schönberg have achieved under Cameron's management, you would end up still talking about two French Jews working in London on shows destined for the world. They are essentially neither French nor British nor American, so that audiences across the world can identify with the emotions and people across national borders. They work, in the same way as Rodgers and Hammerstein worked.

At the beginning of the 1990s, it would have been entirely possible for Mackintosh and his offices around the world just to devote themselves to the literally hundreds of productions of their four big hits. But Mackintosh was far from content just to supervise the empire of tours and foreign premières. In any case, he knew that Boublil and Schönberg were already starting on a third five-year period of development. They had a new musical in mind and they had settled this time on another French subject, the mystery of Martin Guerre. Initially, Cameron was unconvinced that this could ever work on the musical stage. And a few months later, even after he heard the first songs, he was reluctant to accept the premise of the plot.

Instead, his next project was to come from an unexpected source. One evening, with friends, he went to see a tiny revue with an all-black, all-male cast at the Theatre Royal, Stratford East. This little turn-of-the-century East End of London theatre had been the crucible of Joan Littlewood musicals (*Oh, What a Lovely*

139

War!, Fings Ain't What They Used T'Be) and it was also the place where Sondheim had found what would become his *Sweeney Todd* and where Cameron and Lloyd Webber had first seen Ken Hill's *The Phantom of the Opera* that would inspire their own version.

The show that Cameron now saw was called *Five Guys Named Moe*, and was a compilation of the songs made famous by the late great jazz singer and saxophone player, Louis Jordan – not to be confused with the French actor of the same name. Jordan hadn't written all the songs in the show, but the strong rhythms, witty, often hilariously risqué lyrics, and unfailingly melodic rhythm-and-blues-based tunes were all associated with him. A clever writer (Clarke Peters) and director–choreographer (Charles Augins) had hung these songs – which ranged from 'Is You Is or Is You Ain't My Baby?' to 'Ain't Nobody Here But Us Chickens' – on a simple, unforced plot of a boy without a date on a Saturday night, taking his comfort from the radio.

1990 – On a visit to the Theatre Royal, Stratford East (where Lloyd Webber had first got the idea for *The Phantom of the Opera*), Cameron came upon a vibrant musical by Clarke Peters, based on the songs associated with the black American jazzman Louis Jordan. By the interval he had negotiated a deal to bring it to the West End, where *Five Guys Named Moe* ran for the next five years. The Broadway version and subsequent world tours were no less successful.

So impressed was Cameron with the talent and energy of a superb cast and staging, not to mention the material they were so effortlessly raising the ancient roof with, that in the interval he sought out the theatre's producer, Philip Headley, and agreed a deal that would eventually make *Five Guys* yet another of Cameron's long-running hits on both sides of the Atlantic. In every theatre it played, Mackintosh had the sense to try to recreate the drinks-in-the-stalls informality of the original East End version; but, as always at Stratford East, there were still those who believed the show never looked as good as on its first outing.

In these early 1990s, as the realization began to dawn that great shows didn't grow on trees, Cameron, while waiting for the next big Boublil–Schönberg and characteristically unable not to be hugely active, was putting his musicals on the road all over the world. But there were other plans, too. For a start, he had formed the Mackintosh Foundation, a charity that was to set up the first professorial chair of drama at Oxford University and also to fund a National Theatre series of classic musicals, including several Sondheims, notably *Sweeney Todd* and *A Little Night Music*, as well as major revivals of *Carousel*, *Guys and Dolls*, *Lady in the Dark* and, in 1998, *Oklahoma!*

His private life, still a matter of considerable journalistic curiosity, unexpectedly became briefly more public. When, in 1991, Ian McKellen became the first openly gay actor to be knighted, the controversial film director Derek Jarman wrote a public letter of disgust, suggesting that McKellen had no right to accept such an honour from a Tory government perceived by Jarman to be radically homophobic. This complaint, in turn, provoked a brief letter to the *Guardian* signed by a number of distinguished and celebrated theatre practitioners, who had hitherto been open with friends but publicly discreet about their homosexuality. In defence of McKellen, and the freedom of all people to be defined by their achievements rather than their sexual preferences, Cameron was one of the signatories.

Over the next decade, despite many transfers, revivals and small-scale experiments, both here and abroad, there was only really to be one more huge undertaking for Cameron as the hands-on producer we had become accustomed to. But in the run-up to *Martin Guerre*, he suddenly found within himself all kinds of other energies and interests. Having moved to the infinitely more impressive Adam-designed headquarters that his organization now occupies at 1 Bedford Square, he also spent much of this time flying around the world, checking up on all his foreign offices and the musicals that were coming out of them.

If any one thing is to characterize the Mackintosh management (as opposed, for instance, to Lloyd Webber's Really Useful Group, which came badly unglued in the later part of this decade), it is that it retained Cameron's constant and meticulous attention to even the very smallest of details. He would often, for example, be found writing personal first-night cards to the entire third take-over cast of a *Les Mis* in Melbourne or a *Cats* in Cincinnati.

In these years he also came to spend more and more 'quality time' at his homes in Scotland and France with Michael and the very close-knit Mackintosh clan of parents, brothers and friends. It was almost as though he knew that the golden days of the 1980s would not return. 'Let's face it, Andrew and I have been quite incredibly lucky, and if it were all to end tomorrow we could still hardly complain that America and the rest of the world had not given our shows a fair hearing.'

What they had also given him, of course, was the luxury of time in which to pursue other interests. Quite soon he became, with Bernard Delfont, joint owner of the Prince of Wales and the Prince Edward and the Strand theatres in London's West End. The Mackintosh Foundation rebuilt the Old Fire Station in Oxford as a proper performing space for university drama, while also giving money to numerous charities and the development of young musical talent. In this context, always an astute observer of the general climate, he had realized almost before anyone else that if the boom in Lloyd Webber and Boublil–Schönberg was ever to end, Britain would still be in dire need of other composers and lyricists, and they had to come from somewhere. From now on, whether it was the Tricycle destroyed by fire or the King's

Head cut off from public funding, the Foundation came to the aid of dozens of individuals and institutions. Suddenly, in these early 1990s, Mackintosh had become very much more than just another producer of hit shows. His organization had become absolutely central, both financially and artistically, to the future of the British musical theatre if, of course, there was to be one.

In three distinct ways Mackintosh by now had entirely altered the balance of power that had traditionally existed in the transatlantic musical theatre. First, he was almost always sole producer of his own shows – as a look at any current playbill will indicate, it is now not unusual for a Broadway show to have up to fifteen producers. Second, because he had delivered his relatively small team of investors nothing but profit, he now had a queue of others begging to give him their money, and third, as the recent battle over Jonathan Pryce had indicated, he was able single-handedly to defeat these American unions which for years had been calling the tune.

'I am now in the very lucky position of being able to raise $5 million in five phone calls. This has changed my relationship with other theatre owners and producers around the world very considerably. It all boils down to money. Money alone buys you independence. Most really successful projects in the theatre are only initially believed in by a very few people. Very few hits are ever recognized in advance of an opening night and sometimes not even then – it wasn't until (against all advice) I transferred *Les Mis* from the Barbican to the Palace that I could really see any money coming in. Of all the shows I have ever worked on, the only one that people thought was going to be great in advance was *Phantom*.'

The idea of a war between the West End and Broadway, which for several years now the West End seemed to be winning, was always one from which both Andrew and Cameron had carefully distanced themselves. When interviewed, Andrew talked frequently about the crucial influence that the Hollywood film musical had had on him as a child, while Cameron maintained, 'I was just lucky enough to have caught the tail-end of the golden age of Broadway. I grew up with shows like *West Side Story*, *My Fair Lady*, *How to Succeed*..., and then I met up with Andrew and the musical went into an apparently European era. But you have to remember that the great Broadway writers from the 1920s until the 1960s either came as children from Europe or were heavily influenced by especially Jewish European music. America was the great crucible of their talent, but the problem now is that the infusion of talent has not properly regenerated. The great American writers of musicals were popular tunesmiths, with instant radio hits all over the country. In Europe, popular music was more influenced by rock, and the success that we all first had in London was because Tim and Andrew assimilated the sound of pop and put it back into the theatre. None of us now know what will turn the public on, but I can tell you it is certainly not to do with nationality; nobody buying a ticket to *Cats* on Broadway does so because it is British, they go because the show works and it really is that simple.'

Nevertheless, neither Cameron nor Andrew were entirely oblivious to the possibilities of Hollywood where, until a run of catastrophic movie flops in the late 1960s, all great musicals had traditionally ended up. Here, unusually, they were both to prove unlucky, at least at the outset. It took twenty years to find a screen *Evita* in Madonna; *Cats* has only just made it to video; the screen casting of *Phantom* is at this writing still proving imponderable and as for *Les Misérables*, although Alan Parker is only one of several directors who have been allied at various times to the project, there is still not

143

Oliver!
GET HIGH!
CATS
FOOD, GLORIOUS FOOD!
8 DECEMBER 1994
Les Misér
DEUTSCHES THEATER
Der Musical-Hit
I'M A CATS LOVER
GO UNDERGROUND BY
RIVATE CARRIAGE ON THE VICTORIA LINE
OR A COMPLETELY VICTORIAN EVENING!
XFORD CIRCUS – ST PANCRAS
ONE WAY ONLY
8TH DECEMBER 1994
PLEASE RETAIN THIS TICKET FOR YOUR
FREE TRANSPORTATION TO THE PARTY
– ONLY 3 STOPS –
(JUST 4 MINUTES AWAY)
ON THE MAT
The Phantom of the Opera
10TH BIRTHDAY CELEBRATION
MENU
WINTERGARDEN THEATRE
1634 B'WAY AT 50TH ST.
CATS
6:00 PM THU
PARTIAL VIEW

the faintest sign of an actual film, and that goes for *Miss Saigon*, too. On this score, things may improve after the millennium. The success of *Evita* on film appears, at long long last, to have regenerated Hollywood's interest in the possibilities of the musical film.

The theory that *Les Misérables* could do no wrong, lose no money wherever in the world it played (and the total is now somewhere over forty productions and still counting), received in 1991 one short sharp shock. At that moment, the one major European capital not to have had the show (unless you count a pre-Cameron Palais des Sports version) was the home town of both its composer and lyricist, and of Victor Hugo, its original author. Paris, of course. Surely now, with not only Victor Hugo but also Alain Boublil and Claude-Michel Schönberg able to assert proprietorial status on it, the show would break through the legendary French resistance to musicals? Not at all. *Les Mis* in Paris, like *Cats* before it, closed after barely eight months, losing most of its capital despite rave notices and fervent audiences. Not even for three of their favourite sons would Parisians go to see a musical in a city where it had never been chic to do so.

The party is not over yet. All through his career, Cameron has been famous for some of the most extravagant and sometimes eccentric parties in celebration of his musicals' many anniversaries. These are menus and messages from just a few of them.

14

A WHALE OF A MISTAKE

'Three years at sea and still no sign of Dick'

Left – Julie Andrews with the cast and crew in her first return to Broadway in thirty years: Cameron and Stephen Sondheim's *Putting it Together*.

'I have no reason to believe that I'll continue to find new shows as I have in the past'

In hindsight it might be possible to suggest that the failure of *Les Misérables* in Paris struck a warning bell for the new decade. Just as the 1970s had been the decade of exploration and the 1980s that of utter triumph for the four big Mackintosh shows (two by Lloyd Webber, two by Boublil–Schönberg), the 1990s were to end in a kind of meltdown – namely, the economic collapse of Lloyd Webber's Really Useful Group and the painful realization for Cameron that not even he could buy enough time and attention for *Martin Guerre* to survive in the West End at least for the first time around.

But all of that was still some eight years away. For now, Cameron's only real problem was of his own making. Unlike Lloyd Webber, whose talent for management always came a poor second to his gifts as a composer, Mackintosh had now set up a worldwide network of enormous efficiency. In every city where his shows played he had created highly skilled management teams. At home and abroad he took to giving large anniversary parties on every occasion, and more and more of his time would now be spent in Provence (where he had developed a thriving vineyard) and in Scotland where the minimal comfort of his croft appealed to his Puritan nature. Indeed, the richer he got, the less inclined he seemed to be to live like a millionaire. Unlike Lloyd Webber, he managed, between shows, to lead with Michael Le Poer Trench a remarkably private life and, again unlike Andrew, he was able to inspire teams of loyal workers around the world, all of whom formed protective barriers whenever he wished to disappear behind them.

So Cameron eagerly looked forward to a new show and knew that one was slowly emerging from Boublil–Schönberg, but he, had some doubts as to whether it would turn out to be something he wanted to produce. In the meantime his interests seemed now to fragment. The next few small-scale shows he was to present veered from nostalgic revivals and anthologies to rough, and often not entirely ready, experiments. Moreover, with the Mackintosh Foundation getting ever more widely involved in everything from National Theatre musicals through young songwriter schemes and the Oxford Professorship, there was, for the first time, a sense of treading water. Everything was going well, but not necessarily forwards.

One option that Cameron thought about was the chance to go public. Lloyd Webber had asked Mackintosh to join him in a combined venture when he decided to take RUG to the market. Cameron considered this seriously but finally declined. Although his shows were expected to gross more than $150 million worldwide in the 1990s, he had always believed that his independence was priceless. That way, if he chose to give $4 million to charity, or to turn part of the *Miss Saigon* profits over to the homeless in Vietnam, there would be no board of directors or even shareholders to object. In the light of Lloyd Webber's rollercoaster stock market experiences and temporary loss of control over his own assets, this was in retrospect a sound decision.

At this time, it was his regular choreographer, Gillian Lynne, who best summed up the two sides of the man that the American press were now calling Big Mac. 'He can be very impatient with people, and I have sometimes seen him make bad casting mistakes; he's hard to deal with financially, he has a steel shark-like quality; but for all that, if I got into any kind of trouble, Cameron is the first person I would always call.'

Even while the show that would become *Martin Guerre*, as big a production in approach and financial commitment as any of his mega-hits, was in development, Cameron was already speculating that his days as a producer of blockbusters were already almost over. 'I have no reason to believe that I'll continue to find big new shows as I have in the past. These things go in cycles and I'm still young enough to go round the cycle again with a new genera-tion of writers. And if they don't come along maybe I shall just keep on putting on classic revivals and keep the old shows going wher-ever I can. The day I get bored of them I shall stop.'

For someone who was told at drama school that he had the 'smarmy ways of a front-of-house manager', Cameron was later to revolu-tionize front-of-house management, so that there, too, his influence was everywhere in evi-dence – from the first poster in the lobby to the last ticket sold over the phone by an unusually friendly box-office computer system. It was precisely because he was the first person to regard theatre management as involving every single aspect of housekeeping, bar pricing, pro-gramme selling and audience satisfaction, that his influence has always been unique front of house as well as backstage.

And it wasn't even as though he had 'gone Hollywood'. His total London staff was still under fifty, in age and number, and unlike Lloyd Webber or Tim Rice he was still showing only a very minor interest in getting any of his shows on film.

The first of Cameron's 1990s productions could almost be seen as a declaration of war on those who thought he was now only inter-ested in the five-year genesis of potential block-busters. Through his interest in Oxford Univer-sity, which had already had Stephen Sondheim as the first Mackintosh Visiting Professor of Drama and Musical Theatre, he also got involved in the restoration of the workshop space at the Old Fire Station. In New York, preparing for the opening of *Miss Saigon*, he listened to one of the hundreds of tapes which pour into his office daily from aspiring writers of musicals. Unusually, as he doesn't often like pop music in the theatre, the idea and the score appealed to him. He left a message on the writer's answerphone saying that although he had no interest in producing it himself, he would give Robert Longden £25,000 to mount the show at the Old Fire Station. Not surpris-ingly, Longden thought one of his crueller friends was playing a particularly hurtful joke on him, so when Cameron rang back a few days later he had great difficulty accepting that the offer was genuine.

The show was truly weird: a musical of *Moby Dick*. It set up a bunch of alarmingly anarchic and nubile schoolgirls (very like the infamous St Trinian's of Ronald Searle's classic cartoons and films), determined to stage Herman Melville's tale of the big white whale in the school swimming pool. A mixture of high camp, music-hall smut and wild anachronism, *Moby Dick* just about got by as an end-of-term romp with the veteran cabaret star Tony Monopoly playing in drag the headmistress role that had always gone on film to Alistair Sim. He/she played Captain Ahab with a cricket bat for a leg, uttering such classic pan-tomime one-liners as 'Three years at sea and still no sign of Dick'.

Cameron's next contact with *Moby Dick* was when he arrived at the dress rehearsal in Oxford, expecting a cast of twelve and an upright piano. Instead, Longden (who describes himself as 'the Cecil B. DeMille of the Fringe') had expanded and expanded until

they now had a cast of thirty and a band of six. With a score by Hereward Kaye, *Moby Dick* quickly became a cult success among Oxford undergraduates. But Cameron and the show's creators were almost alone in believing that it could possibly have any kind of afterlife, although there were several theatre managers who, caught up in the fun of the small-scale mayhem, offered their theatres for transfer. Against all advice, not only from critics but also from most of his own staff, Mackintosh insisted on transferring *Moby Dick* to the cavernous and wildly unsuitable Piccadilly Theatre because, in its larger incarnation, it could only have broken even in a 1,000-seat theatre. Predictably, it ran into some of the worst reviews he had ever endured.

Two views of this fiasco could now be sustained. Either *Moby Dick* was simply a rich man's eccentric toy, the kind of thing Ludwig of

Bavaria might have organized as a court pageant, or, and more plausibly, that with it Cameron was sending out a deliberate message to the effect that he was no longer just the blockbuster man waiting every five years for a guaranteed hit. From now on he wanted also to get involved in small-scale and sometimes dangerous projects, reminiscent of his earliest days in management. Either that or it was just a plain error of judgement – he had found the original *Moby Dick* at Oxford to be fun and what he had always most wanted in life was for others to share in his fun. Trouble only arose when other people's definition of fun was no longer entirely in line with his. 'I have always got a sense of exhilaration in finding a subject which can take the audience on a trip. I believe that a good musical should be like a roller-coaster – you take the audience on a ride and deliver them an experience they couldn't have

1991 – A whale of a tale, Cameron's next production was a bizarre schoolgirl rendition of Herman Melville's classic *Moby Dick*, as it might have looked in an end-of-term production at St Trinian's. The show opened in Oxford, sailed uneasily to the Piccadilly Theatre, and soon went down with all hands, although there have been recent sightings of a new version well afloat in America.

scale musical of considerably more promise. Through his involvment with the Vivian Ellis Awards for young songwriters, awards that had first alerted him to the talents of Charles Hart who co-wrote both *Phantom* and *Aspects of Love*, Cameron that same year had also found a young composer–lyricist team, Anthony Drewe and George Stiles.

'I fell in love with them because they were the first young writers I'd come across who seemed to me part of the great British music-theatre tradition, which in a way neither Andrew and Tim nor Alain and Claude-Michel really are. Essentially those four are all trans-atlantic in their appeal, but Drewe and Stiles belong much more to the line of Gilbert and Sullivan, Flanders and Swann, and even Noël Coward. When I first met them they had already been together for nearly a decade since college, and they were working on an adaptation of Kipling's *Just So Stories*, which I began to try out first at the Watermill in Newbury.' Directed by Julia McKenzie, it found a very young and untried new performer, Linzi Hateley, who had first been seen when barely fifteen in the disastrous and short-lived *Carrie*, her first starring role. She has gone from strength to strength, as the narrator of Stephen Pimlott's smash hit version of *Joseph and the Amazing Technicolour Dreamcoat*, and a memorable Eponine in *Les Mis*. She is now one of the West End's up-and-coming stars. In all Cameron's career, although expert at spotting crowd and chorus talent and brilliant at identifying production personnel who would shine in his musicals, he has only really made stars of surprisingly few. Michael Ball (*Les Mis)*, Julia McKenzie (*Side by Side by Sondheim*), Lea

found anywhere else. Whether that experience is to laugh or cry is immaterial, as long as they get some kind of an emotional shot. In the end, there are only about a dozen major musicals that are always worth reviving, and they have survived because at their root is a basic truth about the goodness of human nature; they all show ordinary people surviving and flourishing, and that's what makes them immortal.'

Moby Dick failed those tests on almost every level, but even Mackintosh can still learn. What he learned in this case was that Fringe shows, no matter how entertaining, rarely sit comfortably behind a big West End proscenium, just as *Little Shop of Horrors* had never quite worked in the Comedy Theatre a few years earlier. He had briefly forgotten his own cardinal rule about matching the show to the theatre and environment.

Cameron's next project was to be a small-

A NEW MUSICAL BY
GEORGE STILES & ANTHONY DREWE

Musical Direction by KATE YOUNG
Arrangements & Musical Supervision by
MARTIN KOCH
Sound by JULIAN BEECH
Lighting by HOWARD HARRISON
Designed by KENDRA ULLYART
Choreography by ANTHONY VAN LAAST
Directed by MIKE OCKRENT

A CAMERON MACKINTOSH/
TRICYCLE THEATRE PRESENTATION

BOX OFFICE 071 328 1000

269 KILBURN HIGH ROAD NW6

1990 – 'In the high and far-off times, the elephant, O Best Beloved, had a bulgy nose as big as a boot.' Rudyard Kipling's classic animal stories became a musical called *Just So*.

Salonga (*Miss Saigon*), Colm Wilkinson (*Les Misérables*) and Ruthie Henshall in just about everything. These are the obvious examples, but elsewhere the stars of a Mackintosh show are nearly always to be found in the production team and not under the arc-lights.

Just So, a charming collection of songs about Kipling's animals, has yet to find the cohesion that would turn it into a fully fledged West End commercial show. Cameron, despite two try-outs, decided it needed more work, and it is still being readied for its final leap on to Shaftesbury Avenue. Every time it turns up somewhere on the Fringe like the Tricycle or in

the regions, it is clear that everybody is still regarding it as a work in progress. Indeed, having seen it at the Tricycle, Stephen Spielberg bought the film rights to animate the project and the material developed for this film has now been incorporated into the upcoming American staging.

If there was any real secret to Cameron's success he certainly is the last to want to know it: 'I have always loved really quirky shows, but on Broadway quirky is unusual and even in Britain the demand is for something more mainstream. Nobody can define the mystery of musical success but it is clear that (with the

Just So by George Stiles
and Anthony Drewe,
which Cameron has
commissioned and
nursed and guided for
ten years, through
productions at home and
abroad. It remains a
work in progress and
development.

coming of cheap air travel) tourists are more likely to flock to shows with a synthetic global culture. What really appealed to me about *Moby Dick* was its sheer madness and its outsider quality. I had recently been on a trip to the Antarctic where man feels a total outsider.' Even on that holiday, however, Cameron never left the theatre far behind him. On the final night of the cruise, he persuaded the entire ship's company to dress as penguins and perform his least-known show, a one-night cabaret called *Icecapades*.

Meanwhile, at the more academic end of the scale, he now convinced Ian McKellen, fol-

lowed by Alan Ayckbourn, Peter Shaffer and even Arthur Miller to succeed Stephen Sondheim into his Chair of Drama at St Catherine's College, Oxford, as have more recent Professors such as Sir Richard Eyre, Lord Attenborough and the indomitable Thelma Holt.

Cameron had learned that sometimes his enthusiasms worked better away from the bright lights and high costs of the West End. The moment he puts his name on any London poster, expectations go shooting through the roof and it was clear that many of his small-scale experimental interests fared much better without the usual kind of media hype.

Cameron was coming to realize that he could often be more useful behind the scenes or in some kind of co-producer role, where appropriate, and he was by no means convinced that every new show he took on had to be at the cutting edge of experiment or novelty. Indeed, his next two productions were in fact both to be distinctly nostalgic.

Ever since he had first staged *The Card*, back in 1973, as one of his earliest commissions, it had always been a favourite, despite its flaws. Tony Hatch and Jackie Trent had moved to Australia soon after, and Keith Waterhouse and Willis Hall had engaged on other play writing projects. So it wasn't until 1992 that Jill Fraser at the Watermill at Newbury gave Cameron the opportunity to reassemble the team, adding to it some additional songs by his newly found Anthony Drewe.

In New York, at about the same time, Cameron was reviving another old partnership. Starting with *Side by Side by Sondheim* and moving on ten years later to the London première of *Follies*, Mackintosh had always maintained his close links with Stephen Sondheim, close enough to persuade him to be his first Oxford professor with master-classes at which the likes of Stiles and Drewe and Kit Hesketh-Harvey were given unique access to Sondheim's working methods. This begat a series of workshops now known as the Mercury Theatre, one of the crucibles of new musical writing in Britain.

And there was now a still more ambitious Sondheim–McKenzie–Mackintosh plan. Ever since their collaboration on *Side by Side,* it had been clear that another Sondheim anthology would be required, especially as *Side by Side*, although still in regular revival around the world, stops on the very edge of *Sweeney Todd*, thereby leaving at least half of Sondheim's scores unrecalled. For some time Julia McKenzie had been asking Sondheim to allow

her either to update *Side by Side* or to do another version. Sondheim, while not averse to the idea in principle, wanted time to write a few more scores before he permitted a new show to be created. Finally, in 1993, he agreed and, with Julia, devised a new anthology which, unlike the first, would have some semblance of a plot, in fact a New York dinner party within which another twenty or so of Sondheim's songs could be given some kind of context and continuity.

Cameron, cogitating on his dream casting, picked up the phone one day and called Julie Andrews, who had not worked on Broadway in the thirty years since *Camelot*. As it happened, she had decided to return to the stage for her director–writer husband, Blake Edwards, in a new musical version of one of their movie hits, *Victor/Victoria*. Cameron eventually persuaded Julie that before risking Broadway, she dip her toe into the water with a Sondheim anthology in a small off-Broadway house. Here, because of the revue format of *Putting it Together*, she would sing some great songs as part of an ensemble and therefore not have to carry the entire evening alone. This would make rather gentler demands on her than the upcoming, go-for-broke transvestite epic for Blake.

Julie agreed. From the moment the revue went into rehearsal at the Manhattan Theatre Club, it was clear they had a standing-room-only sell-out. Not only was this the first chance to see the star of *My Fair Lady* on a New York stage in three decades, and in Sondheim yet, but her prior commitment to *Victor/Victoria* necessitated a limited sixteen-week season, sold out on the day the box-office opened, on the coldest day of a bitter New York winter.

Putting it Together took its title from the great song in Sondheim's *Sunday in the Park with George*, where the painter Seurat's faithful model sings of the difficulty of making an artistic masterpiece. The show opened on

Side by Side – The sequel. There was a need for a celebration of the more recent Sondheim scores and Cameron, together with Julia McKenzie, one of the original *Side by Side* stars, came up with *Putting it Together*. From left to right: Stephen Collins, Christopher Durang, Julie Andrews, Rachel York and Michael Rupert.

155

1 April 1993, with a cast also featuring the playwright Christopher Durang, Stephen Collins, Michael Rupert and Rachel York, a starry young discovery who was to go on with Julie to *Victor/Victoria* and steal many of the generally unenthusiastic reviews. The notices for *Putting it Together* were, by contrast, a kind of critical love-in, in which the only complaints were that Julie herself didn't have nearly enough to do.

The show was originally planning to transfer to Broadway but the production of *Victor/Victoria* was suddenly accelerated and Julie's first commitment had been to that. So the Sondheim closed and Cameron immediately

began to think about a London *Putting it Together*, starring Julie's best-friend, the American comedienne Carol Burnett. She unfortunately had to withdraw due to ill health, and only in 1998 has Cameron been able to put *Putting it Together* back together, all being well, in a new production for Burnett, especially devised for her by Sondheim himself.

15

FORTUNES OF WAR

❝The returns of Martin Guerre❞

Left – Please, sir, I want some more: Cameron's epic Palladium revival of *Oliver!* (1994).

❝Poverty, abuse, drunkeness, crime, delinquency, death, as well as love, sex, faith, constancy❞

In one sense, everything that Cameron had recently been doing, from the Sondheim revue to *Just So*, was important; but what he was really doing, of course, was waiting for the third Boublil–Schönberg. Before that could get properly under way however Cameron had a lot of work in other directions.

Five Guys Named Moe transferred to New York, where the critics singularly failed to understand that it was an American creation written and performed by Americans in London, and complained bitterly over columns of newsprint, radio and television that the upstart Brits had done it again. They had invaded New York with a British show that lifted songs that properly belonged in American mouths. A good deal of wasted outrage did not, however, stop audiences in New York and else-where from cheering the show nightly. In Miami, where the audience is predominantly retired and Jewish, the management of the theatre begged Cameron to cut the finale of act one, an audience participation conga called 'Pushke Pishky Pie'. He explained that his audience would not be able to dance and the number would fall flat. In the event, there was zimmer-frame gridlock in the aisles, as delirious blue rinses danced their hearts out.

While Cameron was in New York, his plans for the first musical under the major grant made by the Mackintosh Foundation to the National Theatre began to come together. When the idea for the £1 million grant had been discussed among Cameron, David Aukin and Richard Eyre at the National Theatre, and his current director and National Theatre regular Nicholas Hytner, it was agreed that the money should be used for important musical theatre revivals,

The Mackintosh Foundation was set up to encourage new work, help theatres in economic crisis and organize the first ever Oxford Chair of Drama and Musical Theatre. It also gives an annual donation to the National Theatre to allow it to stage musicals that would normally remain outside its budget. Among these have been *Sweeney Todd, Lady in the Dark,* the revived *Guys and Dolls, Carousel* and the current *Oklahoma!*

shows that were worth reviving, not just 'revisi-cals'. They decided that, if the rights could be available in the correct manner – that is, with-out the usual artistic restrictions imposed by the Rodgers and Hammerstein estates – the first show would be *Carousel*. Cameron had seen a somewhat revised version in the early 1980s at the Manchester Royal Exchange, and was aware of the possibilities of a musical which did not disguise or minimize the power of the story.

Hytner was, after all, despite his successful opera debut and his musical interests, first and foremost a drama director. What he saw in this musical adaptation of the Ferenc Molnar tale

was pure drama. Here, in this story of small-town New England, he found the human conditions he knew how to handle – poverty, abuse, drunkeness, crime, delinquency, death, as well as love, sex, faith, constancy – and all the other joys and troubles associated with being young and poor.

Now Cameron met with the surviving Rodgers and Hammerstein family through Ted Chapin, who runs the Rodgers and Hammerstein organization, and they hammered out an agreement. The most difficult point of these negotiations was Cameron's determination, on behalf of the National Theatre, that Agnes de Mille's choreography, which had always been included in any licence deal, would be omitted from this one. Before the family would agree, Cameron had to specify the choreographer who would make the dances for the National Theatre production. He had recommended Sir Kenneth Macmillan to Andrew Lloyd Webber for the staging of his *Requiem* in America, and he now suggested that Hytner meet with him about *Carousel*. They met,

the young director and the senior choreographer, and started work together.

Tragically, Macmillan died during the last rehearsals and his dances were completed according to his sketches. His ballets, particularly the *pas de deux*, were much admired by many critics. *Carousel* opened to enormous acclaim at the National and transferred to the West End, on to New York's Lincoln Center, and then toured the United States and Japan.

There was now one last debt to his own past that Cameron wanted to repay. Some thirty years earlier he had started out as an assistant stage manager on *Oliver!* Indeed, his 1977 revival had been a carbon copy of the original Donald Albery production, using the brilliant

Sean Kenny design which had revolutionized stage settings. Cameron had first come across Kenny's work when he was still a schoolboy, and he was entranced by his unique ability to make a theatrical space dramatically exciting. He would follow Sean Kenny's designs into any theatre, even into the Royal Opera House for *King Priam* where the Michael Tippett music bored him, but Sean Kenny's sets amazed him.

Mackintosh had become the management of the first-class rights of *Oliver!* around the world on behalf of the owners, Southbrook. (Some ten years later, planning an all-new production, he became a 50 per cent owner of Southbrook.) He toured a revival for them until the early 1980s, but slowly he came to the conclusion that, with

Cameron Mackintosh's 1977 revival of *Oliver!* Fagin was played by Roy Hudd at the Albery Theatre and later by Ron Moody at the Aldwych.

classic score, in rather the same way that nobody talks about a 'revival' of *Carmen*, there is just a new production of it. He refused all other requests for productions for nearly ten years, so that when he did decide to put it on, it would be completely fresh.

In 1994, the moment arrived. Cameron met Sam Mendes, a young director who was making his name first at Chichester, then in London at the Donmar Warehouse. Mendes, like Mackintosh, had loved *Oliver!* since childhood, and once again Cameron followed his instinct to give a young director his first big musical. Cameron had to wait until Andrew's successful revival of *Joseph and the Amazing Technicolour Dreamcoat* finally left the London Palladium and then everything fell into place. Jonathan Pryce, whom Cameron had introduced to musicals in *Miss Saigon*, agreed to be the first major London Fagin since Ron Moody, and a vast production was duly built around

the recent death of its director, Peter Coe, *Oliver!* was destined to become a pale shadow of its vibrant original 1960 production unless he could find a way to revitalize it. He realized with increased familiarity that it was in fact the sets which dictated the direction of the show, and however wonderful they were, only when they had been replaced could a new director give the show a new life. As a result he decided to ask the show's owners to rest *Oliver!* for a decade.

Cameron promised himself that one day he would get the musical back in real style, and on a major budget, to the greatest theatre available. He waited to produce his favourite show again until he felt that audiences would not be looking for a revival but a new production of a

Ten years later in 1994, Cameron brought *Oliver!* back to the London Palladium in a lavish broad stage production, which starred successively Jonathan Pryce, Jim Dale, Russ Abbott and Barry Humphries. It ran triumphantly until 1998.

162

"Cameron promised himself that one day he would get the musical back in real style"

him, one that seemed to some of us to be more a celebration of the original than anything closer to the heart of the real thing.

For the original production back in 1960, the three great stars had been Moody and Georgia Brown and the designer Sean Kenny. Since then, there had of course been the musical film by Carol Reed and countless other productions around the world. But Cameron felt that the Palladium stage demanded something bigger, brighter and lighter, which he got in Antony Ward's expansive London sets, even though they meant that the show also lost some of its former emotional and dramatic intimacy.

Oliver! ran in triumph from the autumn of 1994 until the end of March 1998, the longest-running show in the history of the vast 2,400-seat London Palladium. By this time Pryce had been replaced twice by Jim Dale, once by Russ Abbott and once by Barry Humphries. The latter, in a neat quirk of stage history, had in fact started his London stage career in 1960 by playing the undertaker, Mr Sowerby, in the first ever staging of what Cameron has now established as the most successfully revived of all home-grown British musicals since the war. But the most lauded take-over in British theatrical history was certainly Robert Lindsay, who won an Olivier Award as Best Actor in a Musical for a role he had not originated.

With *Oliver!* safely back on its feet, Cameron could now turn all his attentions back to *Martin Guerre* at the beginning of 1995, though it was not to open for eighteen months. Alain and Claude-Michel had delivered to him another draft of their latest score, one they had been developing for several years. The story had been filmed twice in the last few years, first in French with Gerard Depardieu in the title role, and then as recently as 1993 in Hollywood as *Sommersby*, for which the plot was updated to the American Civil War and starred Richard Gere with Jodie Foster as the long-suffering

wife. This was the show about which Cameron had always had considerable doubts. Indeed when the idea first came up, he had worried about the fact that mysteries never totally work on the musical stage since the suspense always seems to be interrupted by the songs.

Of Boublil–Schönberg's three scores, this was always going to be the trickiest; and when Cameron had read what they had initially come up with, he called them in to tell them, with great sadness, that he had decided not to do their show. They were stunned. Alain Boublil in particular found it difficult to accept that, like the record producers they had once been, Cameron wouldn't just hold his nose and produce their work whether he thought it would be a smash hit or not. Cameron pointed out that their many years together had surely demonstrated that his effectiveness as a producer depended crucially on his own enthusiasm for the project. Without that love for the story and characters, he didn't feel able to go forward. They asked him not to make a final decision at this stage, but to allow them to go away and rework the show and bring it back later. Cameron knew he owed them that. Indeed, he suggested they take their baby to Nick Hytner to talk it through with him. Although there was no question of Hytner directing this show, he became the spur that kept them at it.

When Boublil and Schönberg brought it back to him, Cameron allowed himself to be persuaded that *Martin Guerre* need not be a mystery at all. Instead of an ancient French legend turning on whether the Martin Guerre who left a small country village to go to war was in fact the Martin Guerre who returned to it seven years later, they would turn it into a musical play about religious intolerance, the battle of the Catholics with the Protestant Huguenots, and the selfishness and greed of the inhabitants. From the first song the audience would know that the rotten young man who had run away from his new wife seven years earlier had been replaced by his comrade in arms, an altogether better hero for a musical.

Immediately, a familiar problem arose, that of the British 'lyricist'. From the very beginning of their partnership, Cameron's greatest wish had been to establish Boublil and Schönberg in precisely the way that we think of Rodgers and Hammerstein or Lerner and Loewe: and therefore to admit a third writer was always against his better judgement. In the case of *Les Misérables*, Herbert Kretzmer had not just translated Boublil's lyrics into English, he also added a great many of his own. Five years later, when it came to *Miss Saigon*, Boublil's command of English had improved to the point where he and Richard Maltby co-wrote the lyrics in English. Five years later still, this model was the initial plan for the English lyrics on *Martin Guerre*, and once again the search was on for a collaborator.

1996 – Cameron with his mother Diana at Buckingham Palace, receiving his knighthood – sadly only a few months after the death of his father, who had at least lived long enough to learn of the honour.

The usual suspects were again in the frame: Maltby lacked the French background required for this medieval folk tale, and was anyway more engaged in directing and writing than in adding or adapting. Herbert Kretzmer spent some months working with Alain on lyrics, which were eventually rejected because Kretzmer felt that a medieval story should have at least some semblance of period syntax, while Boublil believed that a contemporary musical needed modern language to reach its audience. Cameron was once again in lyricist trouble.

While this search was on, Mackintosh also had to find himself a director for what was always going to be a very tricky project. He was by now determined, as with *Miss Saigon* and the current *Oliver!*, to use someone compara-

tively untested on the broad musical stage, rather than an expert of the Trevor Nunn or Hal Prince variety. For some time he had had his eye on Declan Donnellan, an inventive stage director who, with his partner the designer Nick Ormerod, had founded the Cheek By Jowl touring company for which they had done some remarkably innovative work on the classics, including *Sweeney Todd*. In retrospect Mackintosh realized that *Martin Guerre* was the only one of his shows in which he did not himself pick the designer. In this case, because of the close personal and professional relationship with Declan, the choice of Ormerod was a foregone conclusion.

For a brief moment, Mackintosh even thought he could kill two birds with one stone, and use Donnellan as the English lyricist as well as director, but that didn't work out either. He was instead reminded by friends of Edward Hardy, a young writer who had been one of the prize pupils in the Sondheim masterclasses that Cameron had helped to create in Oxford several years earlier. Hardy had no track record and nothing to prove, and he was delighted to be offered the chance to work with such established writers. As a result, by the time the show finally opened, though Cameron's was still the only name above the title, the credits below it were a monument to the complexity of the process. They read, 'A musical with book by Alain Boublil and Claude-Michel Schönberg, music by Claude-Michel Schönberg, lyrics by Edward Hardy, original French text by Alain Boublil, additional lyrics by Herbert Kretzmer and Alain Boublil.'

One thing kept Cameron's spirits up during *Martin Guerre's* long journey to the stage of the Prince Edward Theatre. His knighthood, announced in the New Year Honours of 1996, was awarded both for services to the theatre and in recognition of the enormous amount of time and money (one overall estimate now

165

❝1996 was to be in many ways the best and the worst year of Cameron's life❞

runs well into eight figures) he has devoted over the years to a variety of charities and needy institutions. Cameron's delight in this honour was particularly poignant because his beloved father Ian, whose strength and support (together with his mother's) had carried him through the lean times, died suddenly, shortly after it was announced. 'But at least,' says his son, 'he lived to see me made respectable.'

A few weeks after Ian's death, Cameron took the Pizza on the Park in Knightsbridge and gave it over for one night to all of London's great jazzmen, who gathered in a unique and joyous tribute to one of their own. There was much drinking, music-making and reminiscing but, above all, family and friends joining to say goodbye in the way Cameron and his family knew Ian would have appreciated the most.

During these difficult personal times Cameron was cheered by the knowledge that whatever backstage troubles *Martin Guerre* was in, the box-office had taken a £1.5 million in advance bookings from the moment the first poster (as always with Cameron's shows, a work of art by the Dewynters agency) had gone up on the streets and in the press.

So it was already becoming clear that 1996 was to be in many ways the best and the worst of Cameron's life. The year of his knighthood and *Martin Guerre* was also the year of his father's death and his fiftieth birthday, and the year in which he made the discovery that just possibly he was beginning to lose the golden touch – as he had predicted he would so many years before. Unlike other producers he was of course still very comfortably cushioned by the four blockbusters still running around the world – *Les Misérables* alone had now played

120 venues – and so secure was he financially that a month or two before the opening of *Martin Guerre*, it was rumoured (as it turned out, incorrectly) that he turned down a bid of $750 million from the Disney Corporation for his worldwide empire.

In that income bracket, the fact that *Martin Guerre* was already overrunning its £3 million budget might have seemed a minor headache. In fact it reflected a curiously unhappy time backstage when everyone from the composers to the youngest member of the chorus seemed aware well ahead of the critics that there was something radically wrong with *Martin Guerre*.

To the outside world Mackintosh was his usual cheery self. It wasn't even as though he was not now as experienced in flops as he was in hits (*Moby Dick* had been useful training there). The problem was his absolute devotion to Boublil and Schönberg, and his conviction that *Martin Guerre* was, no matter what the

Above – Rehearsals for *Martin Guerre* at the Arts Depot with (left to right) Declan Donnellan, Bob Avian and Nick Ormerod. Right – The stars of *Martin Guerre*, Iain Glen as Martin Guerre and Juliette Caton as his wife.

final financial outcome, in its own right a major work. One of Cameron's most endearing, but also from his point of view most dangerous, characteristics is his wholehearted passion for every project he embarks on. Cameron simply falls in love with his shows and it takes a good deal of betrayal or recognition of his own fallibility via the critics or his friends to make him fall out of love again.

One of the ironies of his position was that he had inadvertently created one of his own major problems. By elevating both the costs and the scale of the post-war British musical out of all recognition, he had effectively ruled out the possibility of putting a show on the road before a London opening night. Touring, now, could really only be made to pay with a well-established critical and commercial hit. Despite all this, Cameron wanted *Martin Guerre* to go to Manchester before it came into the West End and was prepared to pay the cost. In this case, it was less of a risk in view of the fact that the previous Boublil–Schönberg shows had run successfully outside London. The problem was that the schedules of his director, designer and the theatre were at odds and it became impossible to find dates that would work.

A brand new show like *Martin Guerre* had therefore to make all its mistakes in previews in London, in front of a theatrically sophisticated audience. People in the business always want to be among the first to see a new show, and they often know what they're looking at, so they are believed when the word spreads, as it can all too easily in the closed and incestuous world of London's theatreland, that something here 'smelt from herring'. In the old days *Martin Guerre* would have undergone its

1996 – The third of the great Boublil–Schönberg musicals to which Cameron has devoted the best part of his last fifteen years is *Martin Guerre*, based on the legend of the mysteriously returning soldier in the Middle Ages, which had already been filmed both in France as *Le Retour de Martin Guerre* and in America as *Sommersby*. The new musical, after much reworking before and after the West End first night, was less concerned with the identity of the stranger than with the religious wars and a small French village in crisis. The show had echoes of both *Les Mis* and *Miss Saigon* but in the end it stood alone as a poetic and heart-breakingly touching account of a peasant community trying to return to work the soil which is its only solidarity.

make-overs miles away from the West End, only coming in to face the critics when it had been knocked into shape.

As it was, the show that opened on 10 July 1996, after a few very shaky previews, was greeted by a generally hostile press. For the third time in little more than a decade, or so it would seem from all but about three of the first dozen reviews, Boublil–Schönberg had written a great and classic musical which nobody liked except the public. When the history of our theatre in the second half of this century comes to be written, it will perhaps be realized that this one team outclassed in ambition and often

home (*Les Mis* and *Martin Guerre*) or abroad (*Miss Saigon*) is quite literally on the turn.

But in a minimalist age, overwhelming epic emotions on the broadest of scales are oddly unfashionable. One of the ironies of the initial *Martin Guerre* reviews is that the show was dismissed as 'Not as good as *Les Mis*' by precisely those critics who had dismissed *Les Mis* in the first place. For those of us who have always believed in *Les Mis*, the joy of *Martin Guerre* was again to hear the story of a community in historical crisis, told through the trumpets and drums and cellos of an orchestral masterpiece.

Certainly, there are times when *Martin Guerre* resembles an unholy wedding of *Brigadoon* and *The Crucible*. The echoes of Arthur Miller and the choreographer Agnes de Mille are in there somewhere, as is *Don Giovanni's* Commendatore returning from the grave, and even of *Macbeth* as three old crones foretold the fate of the hero. But in the end,

achievement even those of Lerner–Loewe or Rodgers–Hammerstein or Rodgers–Hart. What Boublil–Schönberg have given us, at five-yearly intervals, are the operettas of our time: great soaring scores, heart-breaking books and lavish stagings, which bring to rich theatrical life those moments when the history of France either at

Martin Guerre belongs to nobody but itself. Declan Donnellan as director brought the intimacy of his Cheek by Jowl experience to recreate the tensions of an isolated village community, just as Nunn and Caird used their RSC *Nickleby* experience to meet the massive demands of *Les Mis*. What goes on in *Martin Guerre* is an almost mystical sense of war and religion, death and rebirth, deception and redemption. A cripple sings the most haunting lovesong to a scarecrow, even as the misfits of medieval history try to come to terms with an outcast woman whose unborn child may yet prove to be the saving of their community. *Martin Guerre* remains an intimate tale of prejudice and passion, love and other loyalties, and if its central casting was a little uncharismatic (the Shakespeare-trained Iain Glen had trouble reaching the vocal demands of Martin's songs, and, as his wife Juliette Caton had similar difficulty with the dramatic demands of her role), the show itself stands as a monument to the care and nurturing of Cameron Mackintosh and his production team.

But this time the reactions of his friends and even the critics did not fall on deaf ears. Instead of insisting that *Martin Guerre* was in its final shape and everyone who disagreed was wrong, Cameron took a couple of weeks after the generally hostile notices were in to think about what was on the stage and what he and Boublil and Schönberg had originally intended. He came to the conclusion that they had, in the difficult production process, allowed the musical to become too convoluted. The storyline, which had been a relatively simple one, had been complicated by Declan Donnellan into a number of different threads

which the audience had trouble unravelling. The show's opening took too long to come to any kind of point, and the best songs were buried in the choreography.

Unusually, Cameron decided to take a leaf out of the book of his old friend and now rival producer Andrew Lloyd Webber who, a year earlier, faced with similar troubles on *Sunset Boulevard*, resolved by a later and more successful opening in California, had simply closed the West End show down for a period of rewriting and reblocking. Cameron, at a cost of half a million pounds, bringing the total damage to £4.5 million, now proposed to do precisely the same thing. He brought in yet another collaborator, a young lyricist called Stephen Clark, who, like Hardy, had also been a student of the Sondheim workshops that Cameron had financed at Oxford. What Clark decided was essentially that the show needed simplifying. 'I refocused the very beginning on Bertrande, so that the audience knew right away they had someone to identify with and care about. The musical then became her journey through everything that followed.' The cast and crew, committed as always on Cameron's shows to their success, spent weeks playing the original show at night and rehearsing the changes, which included entirely new scenes, new songs, a new ending and a new beginning, during the day. Then, for a full autumn week at the height of the tourist season, *Martin Guerre* went dark to give the technical crew time to retool the show for its changes.

The show reopened on 10 November and was re-reviewed with considerably more warmth by the London press in notices which, with one or two exceptions, still fell far short of the kind of raves that would guarantee *Martin Guerre* the Broadway life still being enjoyed by its predecessors.

The original poster for the first London production in 1996 (left), and the much revised poster for a much revised production of *Martin Guerre* (right), which opened at the West Yorkshire Playhouse in 1998.

16

QUICK FIX

"The family that slays together,
stays together"

'The musical industry Cameron built had overtaken the world but now theatrical times were changing'

No sooner had Mackintosh got *Martin Guerre* up on its feet and running for a second time, than a new storm blew up from quite another and totally unexpected direction. One of the things that differentiates Cameron's productions from other long-running shows on Broadway and in the West End is that he insists that wherever they play, the directors and choreographers make regular unannounced visits to maintain the production values, so that the shows and their casts never look tired or lazy.

John Caird, the co-director with Trevor Nunn of *Les Misérables*, and Cameron, on one of his regular visits to the New York production, which had now been playing to capacity audiences for nearly a decade, saw that several of the actors playing students now looked old enough to be their professors, which is hardly surprising since some of them had been in the original cast. Many had, in the directors' view, now been with the show for rather too long to maintain energy at the regular level of the very first night, something Cameron has always demanded of all his shows worldwide.

Whereas in London, British Equity does not allow actors to be contracted for more than a year, so that *Les Mis* and all Cameron's shows are able to recast regularly to retain their standards, American Equity (Cameron's former jousting partners) insists on run-of-the-show contracts for non-principal roles, specifying that no actor can be fired unless the show closes. Cameron and Caird, in consultation with Trevor Nunn, decided that half the company now needed to be replaced and gave notice to the actors of the action they intended to take. Predictably this started another war

with American Equity, which was no easier than the fight over Jonathan Pryce and *Miss Saigon* had been. This became a serious problem in view of the classification by the union of virtually every role as chorus, a description engendered by the fact that they all doubled in more than one part. Once again he tried negotiating with Equity, once again Equity made a recommendation in private which it withdrew in public, demanding the reinstatement of all the original actors, and once again Cameron called their bluff. He simply paid off the actors he wanted to replace, at a rate far in excess of the amount to which they were legally entitled, and then re-engaged those actors he wished to keep, finding others to fill the roles where he had wanted replacements. The entire enterprise, says Cameron, cost him nearly $2 million.

When that little local difficulty was resolved, Mackintosh returned home. The fight was now on for *Martin Guerre*. In Cameron's view, they had done everything possible, up to and including the drastic reshaping of the show in the light of its original reviews. There remained just one major problem: while audiences liked it more, the wider public were still not going, or at least not in sufficient quantities to make *Martin Guerre* the third arm of the triangle started by *Les Mis* and *Miss Saigon*. From the autumn of 1996 until the autumn of 1997, Cameron fought for *Martin Guerre* as hard as he had ever fought in his life – lavish publicity campaigns, special deals for theatre parties, everything he had ever learned about the marketing of a show was poured into this one. But it didn't work well enough. *Martin Guerre* audiences seldom, if ever, rose above 60 per cent and, at best, the show could just about break even, on a weekly take of around £150,000, but there was no way that the initial investment could at this rate be paid back.

It slowly became clear to Cameron that the story was not perhaps as universal or even as immediately accessible as those of his blockbuster shows, and it was at this point that he began to think about how it could be rebuilt to meet those objections. He suddenly saw that by concentrating only on the main themes, and reducing the overall scale, he could perhaps give *Martin Guerre* a future, both artistically and financially viable. During the run at the Prince Edward, numerous small opera and theatre companies had told Cameron how much they would have liked to have this show in their own theatres, but that it was, of course, too big for all but the West End and Broadway. Boublil and Schönberg had originally wanted to write a medium- rather than a large-scale musical but had, at that time, lacked the experience to pare down their expectations to their essence. Now, with the experience of three major shows behind them, they too understood how this could be accomplished. Like *Sweeney Todd*, Cameron is convinced that *Martin Guerre* will truly find its proper identity in this smaller, more intimate manner.

At this point, the whole British stage musical world that Mackintosh and Lloyd Webber had invented was about to undergo a kind of revolution. Within the last few months, Lloyd Webber's *Sunset Boulevard* had also gone through such disastrous economic times that the whole of his Really Useful empire was now on the verge of total collapse. For fifteen years the industry they had built on just four shows

had overtaken the world. Now that world had suddenly started to show signs of drastic change. In 1997 alone, almost a dozen new American musicals opened on a reborn and revitalized Broadway. The Times Square vacuum that Andrew and Cameron had so brilliantly filled with their own imports had suddenly ceased to exist, and back home there was a feeling that audiences, as they approached the millennium and a new Blair economy, wanted something more than just dancing cats and crashing chandeliers.

Nineteen ninety-eight also saw the closing at the London Palladium of Cameron's three-year *Oliver!* revival, while across at the Lyceum *Jesus Christ Superstar* didn't even make it through to another Easter Sunday. Times were definitely a-changing: the musical world that Cameron and Andrew had dominated for fifteen years suddenly moved its focus back across the Atlantic from whence it had come. In 1997 and 1998 not only did Broadway come back to life with a vengeance, but the shows that were hits in London had reverted to their old Broadway allegiance – 1998 was to be the year of *Chicago* and *Show Boat*, of *Rent* and *Oklahoma!* and countless other imports. The only major original domestic offering was to be Lloyd Webber's *Whistle Down the Wind*, and it, too, had started none too successfully in America, only to open to disastrous press in London.

In fact Cameron had seen all this coming. A year earlier, while still fighting for *Martin Guerre*, he had allied himself with the tiny Donmar Warehouse run by Sam Mendes, who had directed *Oliver!* for him. The show that they now brought to this little and recently rebuilt theatre in Covent Garden was in every way the antithesis of the epic spectacles for which Cameron was famous. A young English teacher in New England, John Dempsey, and an equally youthful journeyman music director, Dana P. Rowe, had scored a surprise hit in the American regions with a weird, off-the-wall cult musical called *Zombie Prom*. It was imported to off Broadway, but failed to find an audience, despite excellent reviews.

But people in the business in New York liked it, including Albert Poland, Cameron's old friend. He now told Mackintosh about the two young songwriters, and they sent him a cassette of their work. 'It contained a score they were still working on,' said Cameron, 'and Tee [Tee Hesketh, Cameron's long-time personal assistant] who usually makes me shut the door between my office and hers when I'm listening, asked me to play it again and again. What they had sent me was the first draft of what became *The Fix*.' Cameron telephoned Sam Mendes and asked him to listen to the tape, and Mendes called back the same day to say that not only did he want it for his Donmar Warehouse theatre in Covent Garden but that he himself would direct it.

Ironically, *The Fix* was to open in Covent Garden in precisely the same May 1997 week as *Beauty and the Beast*. The clash you almost heard was Walt Disney running into Bill Clinton. Clearly *The Fix* still needed some fixing, but for those who liked their musicals by Sondheim out of Kander and Ebb, this was indeed a knife-edged and courageously rock-driven score by two totally untried new Americans, which, unlike almost every other show in town, was entirely original in so far as it had no movie or play or bestselling novel in the background. Or rather, it had several: you could trace the origins of *The Fix* back to such paranoid Washington conspiracy thrillers as *The Manchurian Candidate*, or forward to any sleazy tabloid life of the Kennedys or Clintons.

1997 – Fixing *The Fix*. Another aspect of Cameron's production career has been his eagerness to take a musical still in workshop, or sometimes only in concept, and nurse it through to a small-scale staging. John Dempsey and Dana P. Rowe's *The Fix* is a scathingly satirical White House musical, somewhere half-way from the

conspiracy-theory movies of the 1960s and the violence and bloodshed of Quentin Tarantino. Its initial West End reviews were less than enthusiastic, but since then the show has been ecstatically received in Washington DC and it looks as though, once again, Cameron has a musical which everyone hates except the public.

Indeed, by the end of an increasingly frantic evening, we seemed to have acquired the child from *The Omen*, Marilyn Monroe with that famous dress blown above her waist, and the Mafia, all demanding revenge for the betrayal of their boy in the White House.

As this might suggest, the book of *The Fix* was something of a muddle. It opened with the death of a Presidential candidate and the decision by his widow – a Rose Kennedy figure of startling ambition – that if she couldn't be a Presidential wife, 'bet your ass I'll be his mother'. Aided and abetted by her brother-in-law, a closet gay, wheelchair-bound cripple with a stammer who, in one of the show's many moments of gala bad taste, forces his own nephew to have sex with him, the mother from hell gets her boy within spitting distance of the Oval Office, only to have him then killed, Crucifixion-style, by Mafia gunmen who seem to have stumbled in from some altogether different plot.

The Fix is a black cartoon parody of White House excess and American dreams turned into nightmares. Incest, rape, murder, madness, everything that makes Washington politics so much more fun than Whitehall, are here batched into a manic musical tragi-comedy about a would-be First Family so dysfunctional as to make the Borgias look like the Blairs.

It was a hugely ambitious idea, which needed a great deal more writing and rewriting than it was able to have in a six-week rehearsal period in a small theatre, which nevertheless happened to be located in the middle of London's West End. It is highly possible that, with another six months of development and a couple of out-of-town workshops in the style of *Just So*, it might have been honed and refined into the unusual and different project Cameron thought it could be. Unfortunately, it was launched way too early and let out for the London critics to savage without ever having decided what kind of musical animal it was going to be.

Luckily, that was not the end of *The Fix*. In March 1998 a very different production opened at the Signature Theater in Arlington, near Washington DC, and there *The Fix* finally found its feet as 'the most corrosive, explosive and gleefully wicked musical to have come our way in a very long time' (*Washington Post*). American critics seemed to have no trouble with the style of this still very cynical show, and one local review even reckoned that it had changed the landscape of the musical theatre forever. Lloyd Rose, writing for the *Washington Post*, found it 'a grotesque political cartoon scrawled in primary colors – a pop paranoid version of our worst nightmares about Ameri-

can politics; this is the offspring you would get if you crossed Busby Berkeley with *The Manchurian Candidate*, and it gives you the greatest feeling you can ever get from a musical – that a bunch of talented people were working at the top of their powers and having the greatest fun of their lifetime.'

Signature's resident director, Eric D. Schaeffer, and the original London choreographer, Charles Augins, had clearly now come up with something that had been missing from the first production. But it was hardly surprising that, in the heartland of political America, a show about electing a flawed President, at the beginning of Clinton's second term, should have struck some local chords, which had been harder to hear in the confines of Covent Garden. The peculiarities of the American electoral system were the bread and butter of the very newpapers that reviewed *The Fix*, while the audiences, largely employed by the federal government, had no trouble believing episodes that had been considered preposterous in London.

Back home, while *Martin Guerre* continued still to resist major attempts at life-saving alterations, its run coincided with a marathon series of anniversaries, all of which Cameron could crown with his now famous party-giving talents. Thus were celebrated, within a very few months, fifteen years of *Cats* in London and then New York, a decade of *Les Misérables* in both cities, and the achievement of *Cats* in becoming the world's longest-running musical. Amid these endless celebrations, it was announced that Cameron, alongside Lloyd Webber, Elton John and Paul McCartney, was close to the top of *The Sunday Times'* British Rich list, with a private fortune now estimated at £350 million, just half what *Les Misérables* was said to have taken in around the world.

The triumph of *The Fix* in Washington DC merely confirmed what Cameron had now long suspected, that London critics were not necessarily the final judges of his work, and that the broad-scale shows, just like the intimate ones, could acquire the nine lives of his famous *Cats* in subsequent productions around the world. London journalists were eagerly suggesting that it might all be over. The arrival of *The Lion King* and *Ragtime* on Broadway, and the birth of the new Garth Drabinsky Livent empire in Toronto, all seemed to suggest that the years of the

Mackintosh–Lloyd Webber domination of the world musical might be coming to a close. Cameron pointed out that there were still twenty productions on his schedule for the last year of the century, including revisions, revivals and new compilations all over the world.

'It is purely coincidental,' he told the *Daily Telegraph* in February 1998, 'that I have not got another big show waiting for the West End. Unless I have something absolutely copper-bottomed, or a really major revival, I am now very chary about trusting British critics to smell new talent. I no longer see myself taking something like *The Fix* from left field into the West End – I'm not paranoid, I don't think the press are out to get me personally, but nor do I think there is enough understanding in London of the process of musical theatre for that to be a sensible way of going forward. Most critics from time immemorial are better at listening to old musicals than to new scores, so a revived musical very seldom gets a bad notice because critics know the genre and they know the tunes. The moment they get something they can't pigeon-hole, out come the hatchets. I still passionately believe in the future of *Martin Guerre*, which is why I am already planning a mark three version with some cracking new tunes but a much smaller cast and orchestra, for the West Yorkshire Playhouse. Shows like that can take a long time to come good. Everyone now hails *Chicago* and *Camelot* and *Porgy and Bess*, but none of them clicked at first. You don't write musicals, you rewrite them, and I remain convinced that *Martin Guerre* will one day be perceived as a great popular classic, on the scale of *A Little Night Music* or *Sweeney Todd*.

'If I did not believe I could still find interesting new writing, and eventually make it come good in production, I would get right out of the business. Andrew and I are still the only two producers whose names appear alone above the titles of our shows and as long as I am able, I shall make sure that whatever I do is always mine and not the result of some big-business conglomerate. As Broadway and Hollywood have both proved, time and time again, once you lose the personal touch you very often lose the heart of the project.'

At this point, an interesting and unusually public row broke out between Mackintosh and Lloyd Webber. Andrew, now granted a peerage, suddenly announced that the era of big musicals was over and that Cameron had spent far too much money on *Martin Guerre*. Mackintosh retorted that it was hardly up to Andrew to teach him the skills of musical management, especially as *The Phantom of the Opera* had done notably better in those countries where he had managed it than in those where the Really Useful Group had been in charge.

'Can you believe it?' he said incredulously to the arts editor of *The Times*, 'Andrew's company managed to lose money on *Cats* in Asia and a whole lot more on *Phantom* in Basle. These are incredible shows that have been successful all round the world, and still they lost money. That is symptomatic of how badly managed Really Useful really is. The people who run it simply don't understand theatre, whereas in my office there is hardly anybody who hasn't worked on a stage or backstage. They are theatre people through and through, not managers or economists or the chairmen of boards. It is surely not a coincidence that Andrew's four biggest hits were all done either with me (*Cats* and *Phantom*) or with Robert Stigwood (*Evita* and *Superstar*). The musical theatre, more than any other art form, is a collaboration – an intelligent producer can make a writer write better. Andrew has a little knowledge of production, but he is not a producer and he has surrounded himself with people who cannot fight him artistically. That has been his biggest problem. The one good thing about all

the trouble we have had with the *Martin Guerre* revisions is that they reminded me and the authors and the public and the critics that this business of ours is not a conveyor belt. It's an art form. And I'm in it for the art, not for the money.' This was just as well, considering the way that things were now going. True, the 1997 Olivier Awards did honour *Martin Guerre* as Best Musical (ironically the first time Boublil and Schönberg had ever won it) and as for Andrew, he retracted it all back at his fiftieth birthday party in spring of 1998, acknowledging that Cameron had been right in his views.

By the middle of June 1997, though, much of Cameron's time was still occupied with celebratory concerts for his hit shows and his own half-century, the outside world of musicals was getting decidedly chillier. Lloyd Webber announced that Really Useful's debts were now running at more than $1million a month, and Cameron himself had to face the basic truth that audiences, whether for *Cats* or *Phantom* or *Les Mis* or *Miss Saigon* around the world, would one day dry up. By the end of that summer, Lloyd Webber was talking about a £10 million deficit for his Really Useful Group. 'We are living in the most parlous times I can ever remember. My next show, *Whistle Down the Wind*, will be the acid test. Because shows like *Phantom* have been huge, there has grown up the belief among people doing budgets that there is fat in musicals. Take it from me, there isn't.' Lloyd Webber had now begun to diversify into food columns and his third wife Madeleine's racing stable, but Cameron was very quick to demolish Lloyd Webber's theory that it might all be over. 'My profits were up this year by 22 per cent, last year by 25 per cent and the year before by 17 per cent. Between now and the millennium I shall have fifteen productions opening around the world. The advance for the British tour of *Les Mis* alone is now £7 million. The *Miss Saigon* which

"This business of ours is not a conveyor belt – it's an art form, and I'm in it for the art, not the money"

1998 – Swanning about. All through his career there have been certain productions in which Cameron has taken no more than a godfatherly interest, leaving the original creators (in this case Matthew Bourne's Adventures in Motion Pictures) to remain in total control but with the advantage of a donation from the Mackintosh Foundation, which would allow full realization of the concept. Of these adopted children, *Swan Lake* has proved, in London and New York, one of the most triumphant.

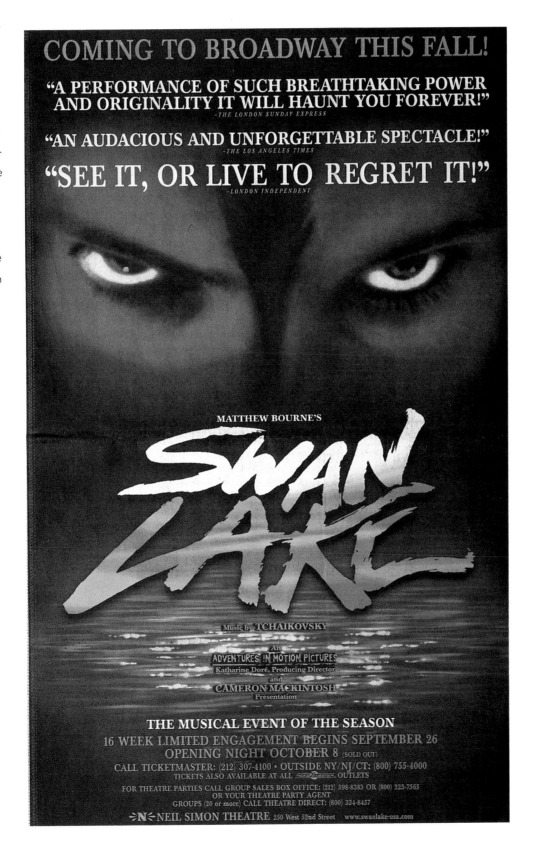

has just opened in Amsterdam will last at least four years, and in Stuttgart it'll be good for ten. I've got five other *Martin Guerre* productions lined up for next year – this can hardly be called, even by Andrew, an industry in collapse or even decline.'

And, as always, he had other irons in the fire. Cameron was now taking a considerable interest in the choreographer Matthew Bourne, whom he had discovered when Sam Mendes had originally suggested him for the dancing in *Oliver!* Never a classical ballet fan, he was none the less persuaded by his colleagues to see a performance at Sadler's Wells of a dance company, well known then only to the enthusiasts, called Adventures in Motion Pictures. The company's founder, choreographer and leading light was a young man who had come to dance too late to be the classical dancer he craved, and too intelligent to settle for the *corps de ballet* anywhere. He began to take the stories of classical ballets and reconfigure them for the contemporary dance audience, who are mostly young and disaffected.

The performance Cameron was taken to was called *Highland Fling*, a very free adaptation of *La Sylphide*. In this remarkably silly story of two other-worldly dancers and their swain, a kilted James, somehow Bourne found a contemporary morality tale involving drugs, marriage and modern relationships. He also found a great deal of humour that would have amazed the original nineteenth-century choreographer, Taglioni. Cameron liked what he saw. He agreed with Sam Mendes that Bourne would be an interesting choreographer for his new *Oliver!* and asked what else he was doing. Bourne told him that he was working on a much more ambitious project, nothing less than an attempt to breach the highest bastion of the balletic art – *Swan Lake*. He would do it, he told Mackintosh, using the traditional Tchaikovsky music but translating the story into a fairy-tale in which

the prince had a mother from hell, a fiancée with a suspicious resemblance to Princess Diana, and where the swans were all men.

When Bourne actually staged this eccentric idea, Cameron, in common with every member of the audience, cried and laughed with the characters and, when he stopped laughing, offered to help bring it into the West End. If that worked, the next step would be Broadway. It worked. For nearly six months, *Swan Lake* was the hottest ticket in town. It had been more than seventy years since ballet had played eight shows a week in the West End, and that had been Diaghilev's Ballets Russes. This time the star was the charismatic Royal Ballet principal, Adam Cooper, who left Covent Garden to star with Adventures in Motion Pictures.

So now there were the Bourne shows (*Swan Lake* and its successor, *Cinderella*) to watch over, as well as the National Theatre musicals which the Mackintosh Foundation had made possible. These now included not only Rodgers and Hammerstein's *Carousel*, which also triumphed at the Lincoln Center in New York, but also such less familiar scores as the Kurt Weill–Ira Gershwin *Lady in the Dark* and the two Sondheims, *Sweeney Todd* and *A Little Night Music*. *Oklahoma!*, the next in the National series, opened there in July 1998 in a production by Trevor Nunn, with choreography by Susan Stroman; and although Cameron is only the nominal head of the Foundation, he has always kept a beady eye on the development of the shows it sponsors, just in case he can transfer them into the West End and beyond.

All the same, Cameron was carefully sidestepping the fact that he was now like a book publisher, living financially almost exclusively on his backlist, while planning for a millennium future in which it was no longer quite so clear what audiences around the world would want. Sixty-eight thousand people in one nation or another were still going every night to a Cameron Mackintosh show, but now minor headaches of one kind or another seemed to be cropping up rather too frequently. In New York, for instance, a woman was suing him as the producer of *Cats* for having, she said, been molested by one of its actors who sat on her lap during a performance, thereby apparently causing her considerable mental anguish. Meanwhile, back in Oxford, the professorship of contemporary drama which he had memorably started with Stephen Sondheim and continued in recent years with Richard Eyre and Richard Attenborough, was now coming under fire – first for its lack of women professors and, secondly, because many of the undergraduates claimed they were finding it difficult to get in to many of the best lectures because of the large attendance of theatre professionals driving up from London for the purpose. An accommodation was soon reached involving larger lecture halls and the appointment in l997 of Thelma Holt as the first female professor – but doubtless not the last.

In a characteristically bullish interview given early in February 1998 to Matt Wolf of *Variety*, Cameron made it clear that the best times might yet be still to come: 'I feel at the moment absolutely at my prime as a producer. I have every intention of taking *Martin Guerre* around the world after it closes in London, and in June I am organizing a gala concert at the Lyceum for charity which we are calling, *Hey, Mr Producer!*, in the presence of the Queen.

'On Broadway, three of my shows are in the top five long runners of all time: *Cats* is first, *Les Mis* is fourth, and *Phantom*, which is fifth, has been the most financially successful of the lot – $335 million and still counting. Of course it remains to be seen how successful these shows are going to be in five more years' time, and I am certainly not resting on my laurels, even if my styles and tastes are not absolutely in harmony with every changing month. For now, my plans include the co-production of Matthew Bourne's *Swan Lake* in New York. Then I plan to put *Oliver!* on the road over here and we are reopening *The Fix* in Washington with a revised score. In the autumn Carol Burnett will lead the Los Angeles première of the Sondheim revue *Putting it Together* which we did off-Broadway with Julie Andrews, and in November at Goodspeed there'll be the American première of *Just So*. Added to all that, *Les Mis* is opening in Antwerp, *Phantom* will go out on tour in Britain, I'm staging the Broadway hit *Rent* all over Australia and I've got a whole new production of *Martin Guerre*, very slimmed down, starting at the West Yorkshire Playhouse and then going on its first British tour.

'In addition to all of the above, *Oliver!* starts another new life in Toronto in January before reaching Broadway in October 1999. *Martin Guerre* will start an American tour at the Guthrie in Minneapolis next year before also reaching New York around the same time, and also for next year I've got the authors of *The Fix* working on a musical of the 1977 Jack Nicholson film *Witches Of Eastwick*. Some journalists seem to think that if you haven't got a London first night coming up you must be unemployed; what they seem to forget is the rest of the country and indeed the rest of the world. For instance the third version of *Martin Guerre* is coming up at the West Yorkshire Playhouse, and there are umpteen more revivals of *Cats* and *Les Mis*, another local tour of *Oliver!* and Carol Burnett opening in Los Angeles in *Putting it Together*, which may or may not transfer. We've recently got *Cats* and *Les Mis* and *Martin Guerre* on video for the first time and there is still the film of *Les Mis* to sort out. So you can see perhaps why I get a little bemused when people talk in the press about it being the end of my musical era.'

PUTTING IT ALL TOGETHER

"Do you hear the distant drums?
It is the future that they bring"

'My gift is for spotting what is wrong with other people's work'

In one way, you could simply tell the story of Cameron Mackintosh via the endless statistics that pour out of his office: 60 million people have now seen *Les Mis*; 7 million in London alone have now seen *Cats*; sheet music sales of 'Memory' are now over 100,000...and on into the millennium and way beyond. But as Cameron has always been the first to note, he is not in it for the money alone. The problem that he now faces is possibly a refocusing of what the public really want by way of a stage musical. Broadway is at last back to its traditional pre-eminence and, for the next few seasons at least, the chances are that there will be a great many more American musicals in London than we have seen since the early 1960s. With backstage Broadway unions at last brought to heel, a major inner-city clean-up of the Times Square streets by Mayor Giuliani and the threat of AIDS at last beginning, albeit very slowly, to wane, the New York theatre is buoyant for the first time in twenty years. There are also big musicals like *Ragtime* and *Show Boat* coming for the first time out of Toronto, thanks to Garth Drabinsky's troubled but highly productive Livent Corporation. Of those who started with Cameron, Tim Rice has made it clear that in so far as he has a professional allegiance, it is to the musical animations of Walt Disney, while whatever the future holds for Lloyd Webber it is unlikely to be on a co-production basis with Mackintosh. Boublil and Schönberg traditionally need five years to get a new score ready for production, and they are both still deeply involved with the reworking of *Martin Guerre*. For them as for Cameron, it remains a work in progress.

For Cameron himself, this has been a time of reflection and re-evaluation: 'A few years ago, when I was in Vienna, I wandered round and there were *The Phantom of the Opera, Cats* and *Les Misérables* and I thought to myself, how could I have ever dreamt that I would have three of my productions running at the same time in one city in Central Europe?

'It was never a matter of having a master plan. It basically went on from *Cats* and we didn't even know what we had there. It was just some settings of T. S. Eliot poems and everyone told me it was Andrew's first really terrible idea. Only much later did we realize that its theme was universal – the tribe and an outsider.

'My gift is for spotting what is wrong with other people's work, and I think perhaps if Andrew had listened to me he might have saved himself some of the mistakes on *Sunset Boulevard*. But I know enough about the history of theatre to be well aware that it always goes in cycles. There is a period in which you learn your craft. You meet people with a similar interest, and for fifteen or twenty years you are firing on all cylinders. Then there is a new audience for something else, and you simply have to recognize when that time comes.'

In the meantime, there was to be another huge project on Cameron's agenda. Late in June 1997, he was approached by the new Blair administration in Britain with the suggestion that he might like to mastermind a spectacular that would form the centrepiece of the controversial Greenwich Millennium Dome.

But it was not to be. Barely six months later, on 23 December, Mackintosh was told that his plan for a spectacular show at the heart of the Dome had been ditched because the estimates were deemed too expensive for the available

Cameron cartooned by Al Hirschfeld amid his leading characters.

budget. For the past few months, Cameron had been working with his designer, John Napier, on a show called *About Time*, which would have involved more than 1,000 children and cost almost a third of the Millennium Dome's entire budget. But the ambitious scale of construction was finally vetoed by the Minister without Portfolio, Peter Mandelson, and, as Cameron said, 'I must admit I am not entirely unhappy. I am now delightfully free of an extraordinary responsibility which was giving me sleepless nights. People are just not used to building multi-media spaces with huge grids and lifts, and the contaminated nature of the site has caused additional problems because its excavation has proved horrendously expensive. Our idea was for a 75-minute show to be performed six times a day, but the sheer logistics of getting 12,000 people in and out of the auditorium were immense. The theme of our show was looking at the future from Britain's great past; we wanted to say to the children that what you learn from the past is what you have to use in taking responsibility for the future.'

As the Dome got into more and more transportation and economic difficulties through the spring of 1998, it began to look as though Cameron had indeed had a very lucky escape. He had insisted on doing the job without any payment, and the headaches would clearly have been enormous.

A few months later, early in June 1998, Cameron was involved in another controversy with the new Blair government and their much-heralded plans for a 'Cool Britannia'. After some deliberation, he withdrew from a £10 million partnership with the Arts Council in protest at its support for 'politically correct' Lot-

tery applications, after he had pledged £500,000 to make up shortfalls in Lottery bids from aspiring theatrical talent. Informally, the word was that Mackintosh felt that some of the projects approved by the new Council were unsuitable and, like many other leading figures in the arts, he was also infuriated by changes at the Council, which had led to the resignation of the entire Drama Advisory Panel, chaired by his current Cameron Mackintosh Visiting Professor at Oxford, Thelma Holt.

Virtually every day supplicants still arrive at 1 Bedford Square with suggestions as to what Cameron should do with his money and, more often than not, they are at least partially successful. Cameron has used his money to rescue theatres suffering cuts in local and national grants, putting a little seed money into countless show proposals, some of which might come good in the fullness of time, while still pouring more money into established theatres, such as the National and backstage charities like West End Cares, than anyone else in theatre ever has. His generosity is legendary and

his willingness to listen to dozens, if not hundreds, of workshop tapes every month remains undiminished. After all, in there somewhere might be a new Boublil–Schönberg or even a new Lloyd Webber.

The story of Cameron Mackintosh thus far has been that of a man who has rebuilt and internationalized the British musical more effectively than anyone in the entire history of our theatre, and as he approaches only his fifty-second birthday that should be our clearest guide as to what to expect of him in the future. If he has a problem, it is one that has existed forever: the comparative shortage of major new musical talent at any one time emerging for and from the British theatre. The reasons, as we have seen throughout this book, are economic and social: the 'double standard' whereby new scores, infinitely more difficult to finance and stage in the West End than a straight play, which traditionally comes in at about a quarter of the cost, are nevertheless treated as second-class citizens, to be approached with caution by backers and audiences alike.

Yet as Cameron embarks on the second half of his producing life, he is in no doubt that it will have to concern primarily new writing. 'If all I could do were glossy revivals, I'd just as soon give it all up and grow wine in France. People may say now that they think we are at the end of the really big, glossy West End musical but I really don't believe that, any more than I believe there are not still some new classics to be found in small theatres and maybe even just on workshop tapes. Musicals are never really going to go out of fashion; it's all a matter of how you manage them. Of course I would give my eye teeth to have a major new musical project come my way, but the truth is that the timing always has to be unpredictable. When that time is right, and the right show comes along, believe me I'll be ready and waiting.'

This then was the mood of the master impresario when, on 8 June 1998, audiences began to crowd into the Lyceum Theatre for *Hey, Mr Producer!*, the celebratory charity concert in the presence of the Queen and the Duke of Edinburgh. Already ticket sales had been so tremendous that an extra performance had to be laid on for the previous evening. But now, as Mackintosh watched the last thirty years of his producing life flash before his eyes, all he knew was that he wasn't actually drowning. That concert has given this book its title (courtesy of Stephen Sondheim); for all of us lucky enough to be there, it was fractionally shorter than Wagner's *Ring Cycle* but vastly more entertaining, a long-overdue reward to the Queen and the Duke of Edinburgh for having had to suffer forty years of Royal Variety performances (Her Majesty was overheard to remark afterwards that if she'd known Mackintosh's shows were this good, she'd have gone to see them before).

This was quite simply the greatest gala of its kind ever staged in Britain. A cast of 200 and an international audience of 2,000 gathered to celebrate the first three decades of Cameron's working life. The company included not only Julie Andrews, making her first appearance on a British stage in more than thirty years, but also Tom Lehrer and Bernadette Peters making their first ever appearances there. There was also an attractively acid little piano duet from the unlikely combination of Stephen Sondheim and Andrew Lloyd Webber, who commented ironically, in songs culled from both their works and with specially rewritten lyrics, on not only the wealth of Cameron's talent but also the wealth of the man himself. (Sondheim said, by way of introduction, that he needed a second pianist for his tribute and had invited the only one he knew who would work for nothing.)

For the rest, it was a roll-call of musical-

*Hey, Mr Producer! –
Cameron's celebration of
his producing life,
brought together stars
from all his shows.*

theatre talent – Michael Ball, Judi Dench, Maria Friedman, Ruthie Henshall, the original *Side by Side* quartet (Ned Sherrin, David Kernan, Millicent Martin and Julia McKenzie, who also staged the evening with Broadway's Bob Avian), Marion Montgomery, Paul Nicholas, Elaine Paige, Clarke Peters, Jonathan Pryce, Liz Robertson, Lea Salonga and Colm Wilkinson.

Two major themes emerged: one was, as Cameron himself noted, that musicals are not written but rewritten, hence we got a preview of some of the new material about to go into *Martin Guerre*. The second was that, when all else is said and sung, Mackintosh and Lloyd Webber are still the only producers with a solo name above the title – like Sondheim's 'Old Friends' (the song which closed the show) and another of his signature tunes, 'They're Still Here'.

They remain not only the best hope for the future of the British musical, but also the only one. Watching this lavish and loving pageant of *Cats* and *Oliver!* and *My Fair Lady* and *The Fix* and *Little Shop of Horrors* and *Godspell* and *Anything Goes* and *The Boy Friend* and *Five Guys Named Moe* and *Martin Guerre* and *Miss Saigon* and *The Phantom of the Opera* and *Follies* and *Oklahoma!* and *Song and Dance* and *Carousel* and *Side by Side by Sondheim* and *Les Misérables* it was clear, in those few seconds

when the cheering stopped, that this was a truly amazing range of work.

The evening was made all the more remarkable by the one thing that nobody seems to have noticed. In order to stage this gala in an earlier time, it would have been necessary for Mackintosh to close all five of his long-running musicals, just so as to find enough singers and dancers to provide the huge choruses necessary. The fact that all those shows played that night is ultimate proof that Mackintosh, his composers, choreographers and directors have now created a British musical community which, for the first time, is in the same league as Broadway in both quality and quantity.

There is no better way to finish this book than with this gala. At the very beginning, a small boy dressed in his best kilt, the same age as Cameron was when he discovered musical theatre more than forty years ago, saw the magic piano of Julian Slade's *Salad Days*. At the very end, Mackintosh himself, identically dressed in his best kilt, standing in the same place, sang the song which had started it all:

'If I start looking behind me
And begin retracing my track
I'll remind you to remind me,
We said we wouldn't look back.'

June 1998 – An all-star concert at the Lyceum Theatre in the presence of Her Majesty the Queen set the seal on the first thirty years of Cameron's producing career. Although it marked nothing more than the halfway point in a remarkably productive career, it is as good a landmark as any with which to bring this book to a close.

190

Cameron Mackintosh – summary of key productions

Space precludes a complete listing of all the shows Cameron has presented since 1967, however we do feature here at least some of the many highlights.

26 June 1967
The Reluctant Debutante
Henley, Kenton Theatre

18 November 1969
Anything Goes
London, Saville Theatre

27 December 1971
Salad Days
UK Tour

27 June 1972
Trelawny
UK Tour, London, Sadler's Wells and Prince of Wales

7 June 1973
The Card
UK Tour, London, Queen's Theatre

24 December 1974
Godspell
UK Tour

4 May 1976
Side by Side by Sondheim
London, Mermaid, Wyndham's, Garrick and UK Tour

26 May 1976
Lauder
UK Tour

16 July 1977
Oliver!
UK Tour, London, Albery Theatre

9 November 1978
My Fair Lady
Leicester, UK Tour and London, Adelphi Theatre

29 November 1979
Oklahoma!
Leicester, UK Tour and London, Palace Theatre

13 May 1980
Tom Foolery
Brighton and London, Criterion Theatre

11 May 1981
Cats
London, New London Theatre

14 December 1981
Tom Foolery
New York, Village Gate

26 March 1982
Song and Dance
London, Palace Theatre

20 May 1982
Little Shop of Horrors
New York, WPA and Orpheum Theaters

7 October 1982
Cats
New York, Winter Garden Theater

12 May 1983
Oliver!
UK Tour and London, Aldwych Theatre

12 September 1983
Blondel
UK Tour and London, Old Vic and Aldwych Theatre

12 October 1983
Little Shop of Horrors
London, Comedy Theatre

11 November 1983
Cats
Tokyo and Japanese Tour

8 December 1983
Abbacadabra
Hammersmith, Lyric Theatre

21 December 1983
Cats
USA Tour No.1

12 April 1984
The Boy Friend
UK Tour, Canada, London, Old Vic and Albery Theatre

13 January 1985
Cats
USA Tour No.2

27 July 1985
Cats
Sydney, Theatre Royal and Australian Tour

18 September 1985
Song and Dance
New York, Royale Theater

8 October 1985
Les Misérables
London, Barbican and Palace Theatre

11 September 1986
Cats
USA Tour No.3

9 October 1986
The Phantom of the Opera
London, Her Majesty's Theatre

31 March 1987
Cats
USA Tour No.4

17 June 1987
Les Misérables
(Tokyo, Imperial Theatre)

21 July 1987
Follies
London, Shaftesbury Theatre

27 November 1987
Les Misérables
Sydney, Theatre Royal

15 December 1987
Les Misérables
USA Tour No.1

26 January 1988
The Phantom of the Opera
New York, Majestic Theater

29 April 1988
The Phantom of the Opera
Tokyo, Nissei Theatre

1 June 1988
Les Misérables
USA Tour No.2

28 November 1988
Les Misérables
USA Tour No.3

25 May 1989
Cats
UK Tour No.1

20 September 1989
Miss Saigon
London, Theatre Royal, Drury Lane

22 November 1990
Just So
London, Tricycle Theatre

31 May 1989
The Phantom of the Opera
USA Tour No.1

2 June 1990
The Phantom of the Opera
USA Tour No.2

8 December 1990
The Phantom of the Opera
Melbourne, Princess Theatre

14 December 1990
Five Guys Named Moe
London, Lyric Theatre

11 April 1991
Miss Saigon
New York, Broadway Theater

29 January 1992
Putting it Together
Oxford, Old Fire Station

17 March 1992
Moby Dick
London, Piccadilly Theatre

8 April 1992
Five Guys Named Moe
New York, Euguene O'Neill

14 April 1992
Les Misérables
UK Tour No.1

5 May 1992
Miss Saigon
Tokyo, Imperial Theatre

23 July 1992
The Card
Newbury, Watermill Theatre

17 October 1992
Miss Saigon
USA Tour No.1

13 December 1992
The Phantom of the Opera
USA Tour No.3

2 March 1993
Putting it Together
New York, Manhattan Theater Club

15 July 1993
Five Guys Named Moe
USA Tour No.1

15 September 1993
Carousel
London, Shaftesbury Theatre

19 October 1993
The Phantom of the Opera
UK Tour No.1

1 August 1994
The Card
London, UK Tour and Moscow

6 September 1994
Five Guys Named Moe
UK Tour No.1

8 December 1994
Oliver!
London, Palladium

26 March 1995
Miss Saigon
USA Tour No.2

29 July 1995
Miss Saigon
Sydney, Capitol Theatre

18 September 1995
Five Guys Named Moe
UK Tour No.2

10 July 1996
Martin Guerre
London, Prince Edward

12 May 1997
The Fix
London, Donmar Warehouse

12 May 1997
Les Misérables
UK Tour No.2

30 March 1998
The Fix
Washington, Signature Theater

7 May 1998
The Phantom of the Opera
UK Tour No.2

7 June 1998
Hey, Mr Producer!
London, Lyceum Theatre

8 October 1998
Swan Lake
New York, Neil Simon Theater